BUILDING FORMS & REPORTS

Using Microsoft Access 2010

F. Mark Schiavone, Ph.D.

D1597199

Sycamore Technical Press
www.sycamoretechnicalpress.com

Preface

Microsoft Access is a powerful database management system. It provides easy to work with tools to assist you in the management of your database. Beyond creating a compact and efficient database, populating it with data, and knowing how to query that data, an Access database becomes even more useful when you add two important user interface objects: Forms and Reports. This book will discuss in detail how to create these two important user interface objects, both by using a suite of powerful Wizards that come with Microsoft Access and by using manual methods. We'll tour the basic form and report types and conduct an inventory of the types of controls used on each.

Forms are the preferred way to enter or edit data in a database. The controls that map to an underlying table or query's fields may be arranged in a manner that supports intuitive data entry or data editing. Forms support **Tabs** which permit you to cluster fields from large tables into more manageable groups. Forms also support **Subforms**, which make the presentation, entry, and editing of related data an easy task. This book will tour all of these aspects of forms and much more with the intent of providing you with the skills necessary to create a suite of forms that will make any database you create using Microsoft Access an easy to use application.

Reports are not interactive in the way that forms are, but are critical to any database that must support decision making or the general business need to review information contained within a database. Reports may be simple lists of select fields from one or more tables, or be much more sophisticated objects that automatically group (up to ten levels) data from one or more tables. Reports also provide the capacity to calculate sub and grand totals and to extend calculations related to field data on the report. Reports are also useful when you need to support mass or bulk mailings and you will learn how to create mailing label reports as part of your report tour.

In summary, Forms and Reports take a database to a new level of usability by providing objects that make data entry, data editing, and data reporting and summarization easy for yourself and/or your end users. In *Building Forms & Reports using Microsoft Access* you will pick up the skills required to create these very useful interface objects.

Manual Conventions

Throughout this manual reference is made to various components of the software. Tabs, ribbons, groups, command buttons, and windows and views appear in boldface type, for example, **OK** and **Font**. Keystrokes appear in boldface italic type, for example, ***Ctrl + V*** and ***Enter***. Throughout this manual you'll find the following helpful items:

Notes of importance, Mouse and/or keyboard shortcuts, Cautionary notes, Best practices, and References to other titles in this series.

Table of Contents

Introduction

This short book is designed to provide the reader with the skills necessary to create a wide variety of forms and reports using Microsoft Access. The reader will learn how to create simple forms and reports that are based on a single table, as well as more complex forms and reports that use two or more tables as their data source. Forms are a very useful data entry and editing tool and make working with a database far easier than working directly with table data. Likewise, reports provide summary views of your data that are not available via tables. Reports also provide the ability to cluster or group related data - in up to ten levels - making reports very useful as data summary devices. In this book you will learn how to create simple and complex forms and reports with the end goal of making your database easier to use and a more powerful analytic and reporting tool.

The contents of this book were originally designed to be delivered in the context of workplace training. When working with staff in a busy corporate or governmental organization I found it important to streamline the approach and design courseware that did not serve as a systematic review of every button you could push in an application. Rather, the approach then, as now, has been to identify and focus on the most important tasks required to get a specific job done. It is my sincere wish at upon completion of this material you'll find that such a task-based focus will leave you with the skills required to design a reliable and easy to use database.

The sample database used extensively in this book is available for download. Point your browser to www.sycamoretechnicalpress.com and move to the customer support area.

A Note About the Views Used in This Book

By default, Access 2010 organizes all open objects as **Tabbed Documents**. In previous versions any open object resolved to an individual **Overlapping Window** within Access. These general views can be toggled and are applied on a database-by-database basis.

For the purposes of creating screen shots of forms, reports, and their design environments this book used the individual window approach. It reduces clutter and creates screen shots of only the element or elements being discussed. The difference between the two views is otherwise minor and if you choose to develop forms and reports and stay with **Tabbed Documents**, the major difference will be in how the title bar for your form or report appears and the fact that your form or report will be anchored to a tab bar rather than permitted to free float as an individual window. To switch between these views choose the **File** tab, then select **Options**. Choose **Current Database** from the list of objects on the left hand pane and select the appropriate option in the **Document Window Options** area.

Chapter 1 | Overview of Forms and Reports

Forms and reports serve as interface elements in the design of a database. Through forms, a user may interact directly with the data by entering or deleting records or by making edits to existing data. Reports present a printed version of the data in the database, often displaying related data in *groups*. In both cases, these objects offer functionality not available when working with data directly in tables and are essential tools when building a database application.

Before embarking on the task of creating forms and reports for a database, consider the following points.

Know the Database Structure

For a form or a report to perform optimally requires a deep understanding of the overall structure of the database.

- Know the structure of the database tables. It is important that you know which fields constitute the primary and/or foreign keys and that you understand the join properties that relate tables.

- Know the field properties for each table. Forms, reports (and queries) inherit field properties which will affect how data are displayed, edited or created. For example, a table field that has both its input mask and format properties set, when added to the design of a form, will exhibit those properties on the form as well.

- Understanding how tables are related also affects report design. The Report Wizard will attempt to group related data based on how the underlying tables are joined.

- Forms and reports will inherit sort orders and filters from tables or queries, if those tables or queries have sort orders or filters applied when the form or report is created.

- Controls on forms and reports will inherit field properties such as format or input mask from a table, or from a query based on the table.

Understand the User's Needs

Because forms and reports serve as an interface between the database data and the database user's needs, it is important that you understand what those user needs are. Note that even if you will be the sole user of the database, following these points is still helpful.

- If you are modifying an existing database, talk to the current users to see what interface elements work well or are difficult to use. Note those components identified by the users as good design elements and work toward implementing those design features throughout the database.

- For new databases, interview the prospective users to get a sense of what their data input and output needs are. Many developers mock up data entry forms to get specific feedback from the users.

- If you are creating a database for one or more other users, interview them to understand their work flow. Your forms and reports should integrate well with how your end users work with their data.

- Analyze current reporting needs by looking over existing reports. Interview the key players who require reports to identify specific reporting needs. For each report, list the fields required, grouping requirements, sorting orders and other important factors. You may find it helpful to create a mockup version of each report and ask key players to critique the design.

Use Consistent Design

Design of forms and reports is an important element of the database design process. A consistent design reduces training efforts and identifies each form and report as belonging to your database.

- For forms, ensure that common objects such as form labels and OK and Cancel buttons are placed similarly between forms.

- Use the same font and font attributes such as text color throughout the forms. Form background color and/or background images should also be the same.

- In lieu of a custom design theme for your forms, base form design on other common Windows applications. Examine how dialog boxes appear in Microsoft Word or Microsoft Excel and use these as design templates. Copying existing common design themes reduces user training since most individuals are already familiar with the forms in commonly-used applications.

- When designing reports, place common elements such as the report title, field or column headings and page numbers in the same location between reports.

- Use the same font scheme between reports. For example, all column headings might appear in 14 point Arial Bold, while the report data is printed in 10 point Times New Roman.

Why Use Forms?

Forms have several purposes in a database application. A form may be *data-bound*, meaning that it is connected to one or more tables and is capable of displaying data for the purposes of viewing, editing, deleting, or creating records. A data-bound form may be connected to a single table, or two or more tables that reflect either a one-to-many or a many-to-many relationship. Further, a form may display multiple subsets of data reflecting several one-to-one or one-to-many relationships.

A form features every search, sort, and order function available to a table. It extends this functionality by offering an array of form controls such as command buttons, drop down or combo boxes, radio buttons, and much more. If the data and controls on a form appear too cluttered, you can organize groups of controls using tabs, or arrange for some data and controls to only appear on pop-up forms. You can also create calculated controls that conduct arithmetic or function operations on some of the underlying data - for example to tally two or more other, numeric fields on the form.

Unbound forms are not connected to an underlying table yet still provide useful functionality. This type of form is typically used to create menu-driven applications so the end user need not know how to navigate your application using the standard **Navigation Pane** and its attendant groups of database objects. Unbound forms may also contain controls and serve as devices to elicit input from the user or to display information not related to table data (such as system or status messages).

Although only touched upon in this book, forms and their associated controls are capable of reacting to a rich set of *events*. You can use VBA (Visual Basic for Applications) program code to define how a form or control reacts to an event. Examples include clicking on a command button to open another form or reacting to when a user attempts to delete data from a text box. Some VBA code will be introduced in this book, but for understanding the full power of using VBA in an Access database application the reader should consider the book *Building VBA Applications Using Microsoft Access*, which is part of this series.

Why Use Reports?

Unlike forms, reports cannot interact directly with the user of a database application. However, as a tool to present formatted, ordered, grouped, and summarized views of data they are indispensable. Although a table can certainly present data (including calculated columns), tables lack the functionality required to display sophisticated grouping and sub and grand totals. Reports may serve to simply format records from a single table, create a sales receipt or summarize and group complex datasets involving multiple levels of organization. Almost all reports in an Access database are data-bound.

Like forms, reports also come with an array of useful controls. Because they are not interactive, objects such as command buttons and combo boxes aren't practical. Other controls such as check boxes (to provide a quick visual on yes/no, true/false data), image controls, charts, and especially text boxes do provide additional functionality. Text boxes in particular are heavily used in reports - for example to display sub and grand totals of numeric data.

Unbound reports are not as common as data-bound reports but they do make the occasional appearance in a database application. Printed instructions, cover pages, and summaries can be created using unbound reports.

Lastly, like forms, reports and their associated controls are capable of responding to a rich set of *events*. This book does contain some discussion of using VBA code associated with reports, but for a more detailed discussion of VBA report programming, the reader is directed to the book *Building VBA Applications Using Microsoft Access*, which is part of this series.

Tabbed Documents and Overlapping Windows

New to Access 2010 is the **Tabbed Document** view. It is applied by default to any new database you create. When any table, query, form, or report is open the object appears as a member of a tab bar. When you have two or more objects open their title tabs appear from left to right across this bar. The currently-selected object will occupy the entire space below the tab bar.

As mentioned in the Introduction, this book utilizes the earlier **Overlapping Document** view which was the standard for Access until the 2010 version. Any open object in this view appears as a separate window. Each window displays a title bar and there is no containing tab bar to contain the open objects. In this view, individual objects may be sized so they overlap or appear side by side. Because this view makes for less cluttered graphics when obtaining screen shots, it's the view that was applied to the sample databases during development.

It's easy to switch between these two views. The style you choose only applies to the database open at the time.

How to Change Document Window Options

Step 1.   Select the **File** tab, then select **Options**. A dialog box similar to the following will appear:

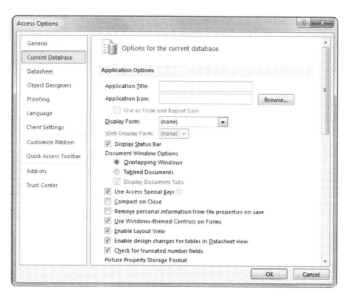

Step 2.   Choose **Current Database** if not selected.

Step 3.   In the **Application Options** area, choose the desired **Document Window Options**.

Option	Description
Overlapping Windows	The classic view in prior versions of Access. There is no tab bar that open objects are bound to. Any open table, query, form, or report appears as a separate, sizable and moveable window.
Tabbed Documents	The new default view in Access. A tab bar contains any open object. When selected, the open object fills the area below the tab bar. No two objects may be open or viewed at the same time.

Step 4.   Choose **OK**.

 You must close and reopen the current database for your change to take effect. One quick way to do this is to select the **Compact and Repair** command from the **File** tab.

Chapter 2 | Overview of Forms

Forms serve a variety of purposes in a database. Good database design uses forms for all major tasks and steers the user away from data entry using tables. Forms may be classified based on their functionality and whether they are *bound* or *unbound* to data..

Bound and Unbound Forms

A *bound* form is connected to a *record source* which is a table, a query or a *Structured Query Language (SQL) Statement* (which is similar to a query but does not appear in the list of queries in the **Navigation Pane**). *Bound* forms make up the majority of forms created in most Access databases since their purpose is to display records for viewing and editing.

In **Form Design View**, *bound* forms have a **Field List** which displays all the fields from the record source. When a field is dragged from this list and placed on a form, it becomes a *bound control* and is capable of displaying values from that field.

A typical *bound* form would appear similar to the following:

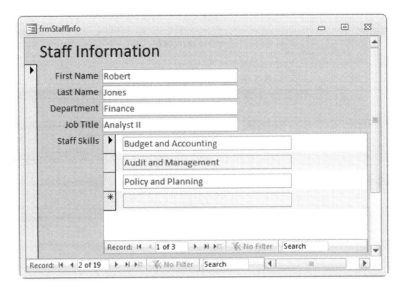

Unbound forms do not have an underlying record source and are therefore not used to display records from the database. Generally, *unbound* forms are used for switchboards and dialog boxes. Any control on an *unbound* form is also *unbound* because there is no record source and therefore no **Field List**.

A typical *unbound* form might appear similar to the following:

A list of form types is presented in the following table.

Form Types

Type	Description
Data Entry	This type of form is the most common in database design. Data entry forms are used to create new records, or delete or edit existing data. All the filtering, sorting, and finding functions Access provides for **Table Datasheet** view are also available to **Form View** as well. All data entry forms are *bound* forms.
Switchboard	A switchboard provides a series of choices for the database user. The choices are usually based on functional tasks such as entering new records or producing reports. These are also called *menu* forms. Switchboard forms are usually *unbound*.
Decision Support	These forms are generally used to view summary data and do not support data entry. Decision support forms may include summaries, totals, PivotTables, PivotCharts, simple charts, or graphs. Managers frequently use decision support forms. Decision support forms are *bound* forms.
Dialog Box	Dialog boxes constitute a large, loosely defined group of forms. They can provide functionality in order to support administrative or housekeeping tasks, or may prompt the user for additional information before implementing a specific task. For example, a dialog box may prompt the user for a date range before printing a date-based report. Dialog boxes are usually *unbound*, although in some designs they may be *bound* to supply choices from a table or query.

Points on Forms

- A central feature of all forms is whether they are bound or unbound to a record source. Bound forms are connected to a table or query and therefore are capable of displaying data for data entry or data lookup tasks. Unbound forms are not connected to a record source and therefore cannot display database data.

- A form that uses a subform to show data from two tables related in a one-to-many join does not need to be based on a query in order to connect the two tables. The form's record source in the table from the one side of the join and the subform's record source is the other table. Special properties ensure that the form and subform are correctly connected via the primary and foreign key fields. Usually, regardless of whether a Wizard creates the form and subform or you create them manually, this property is set automatically.

- When a form and a subform are based on tables joined in a many-to-many relationship, the record source of the subform must be a query that joins the bridge table with one of the primary tables. This is true even when a form is created by a Form Wizard, although the wizard will create the query for you and store it with the form design.

- When a form is bound to a record source, form properties specify attributes which control the nature of the data connection.

- Forms serve as containers for controls. Controls are objects such as text boxes, option buttons, and labels. Like forms, individual controls may be bound or unbound. When bound, a control is connected to a specific field from the form's record source.

The Record Navigator

When working with a bound form (or indeed, when working with tables or queries in **Table Datasheet View**), a **Record Navigator** control appears to assist you in moving through the bound records. The control appears in the lower left corner of a form or subform (it is in the same location for tables and queries as well). The control and its components are illustrated below.

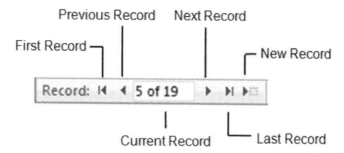

You use the **Record Navigator** to step through a recordset. In most cases you may also use the control to move to a new, blank record. If this particular command is disabled it is because the **Allow Additions** property of the form or subform may be set to *No*, or the underlying recordset does not support the creation of new records (some query types and forms based on many-to-many joins will exhibit this behavior). The current record will display the ordinal position of the record against all records in the recordset. You can use this control, for example, to jump to the 15th record by keying *15* into the **Current Record** text area and pressing *Enter*.

Overview of Form Creation

There are three broad approaches to creating a form in Access. You may create a form using any of the quick form features. The **Form Wizard** can step you through the process of creating a variety of form types, including forms bound to more than one table, or you can create a form completely from scratch (either a bound or unbound form). The following table outlines the various options which appear in the **Forms** group on the **Create** tab.

Form Creation Methods

Control	Description
Form	Creates a form set to display one record at a time, based on the currently selected table or query. The form opens in **Layout** view.
Form Design	Opens form in **Form Design** view. If you add fields from the **Field List** the form automatically becomes a bound form.
Blank Form	Opens a blank form in **Form Layout** view. If a table or query was selected first, the field list for that table or query will appear in the **Field List** window.
Form Wizard	A useful tool to create *bound* forms. The wizard can work with a single table, or two or more tables involved in either a one-to-many or a many-to-many relationship. The wizard will set options such as how many records are viewed at one time, general formatting, etc.
Navigation	Creates a container capable of organizing multiple forms and/or reports. Options set where menus (used to open forms and/or reports) are arranged within the container.
More Forms - Multiple Items	Creates a form set to display multiple records at a time, based on the currently selected table or query. The form opens in **Layout** view. This form is not useful for displaying related data.
More Forms - Datasheet	Creates a form displaying data in **Datasheet** view - essentially a form that appears as a table - based on the currently selected table or query. Forms viewed in **Datasheet** view cannot display objects that may be contained within the form header or footer sections, nor can they display any controls which may be placed in the detail section. This form is not useful for displaying related (i.e. relationally joined) data.
More Forms - Split Form	Makes hybrid form that displays information about a single record in the upper area while displaying a **Datasheet** view from the same table in the lower area. As you select records from the **Datasheet** view the upper area refreshes. The form is based on the currently selected table or query and like other forms in this group are not useful when you need to display related records across tables.
More Forms - Modal Dialog	Creates an *unbound* form that is *modal* (no other objects may be manipulated until this form is closed). The form contains an **OK** and **Cancel** button and opens in **Form Design** view.
More Forms - PivotChart	Opens a PivotChart based on the currently selected table or query. The form is opened in **PivotChart** view.
More Forms - PivotTable	Opens a PivotTable based on the currently selected table or query. The form is opened in **PivotTable** view.

Of all the form creation methods outlined above, the **Form Wizard** is by far the most useful. With the exception of manually creating a form (via the **Form Design** or **Blank Form** buttons), the other forms are configured to work best with single-table data, and several of the form options are just slight variations on a theme. The difference between some of these form types involve specific properties of a form. We'll return to this list of forms in Chapter 4 and, once we've been exposed to form properties, investigate which properties are set by the quick-creation methods listed in the previous table.

As mentioned, **Form Wizards** are typically the easiest way to create a bound form. This includes forms that display information from related tables. The wizard can create forms based on both one-to-many and many-to-many relationships. Many developers first create a form using the **Form Wizard** and then go on to modify the form design manually to add additional functionality or to rearrange form controls and appearance.

How to Create a New Form (Generalized Procedure)

Step 1.   Select the **Create** tab.

Step 2.   Using the previous table (**Form Creation Methods)**, select the desired method. Note that for forms created using the **Form** button, or any of the options from the **More Forms** dropdown (with the exception of **Modal Dialog)**, you should first select the table or query you wish to base the form on.

If you choose to use the **Form Wizard**, skip the rest of this procedure and follow the next discussion.

Step 3.   The newly-created form will open in **Layout** view. Make any changes to the layout if desired.

Step 4.   When you close the form Access will prompt you to save the design. If you choose **Yes** enter a name for the form. Choosing **Cancel** will return to the previous view (without saving the form design). Choosing **No** will close the form without saving it.

Creating a Simple Form using the Form Wizard

Forms that are bound to a single table represent the simplest type of data entry forms. When a form is bound to two or more tables, or to a query which itself displays data from several tables, another layer of complexity is added since the form will typically contain one or more subforms. We'll first investigate using the **Form Wizard** to create a simple form as a good introduction to how the wizard works.

How to Create a Simple Form using the Form Wizard

Step 1.   From the **Forms** group on the **Create** tab, choose **Form Wizard**. The first dialog box of the **Form Wizard** will appear similar to the following:

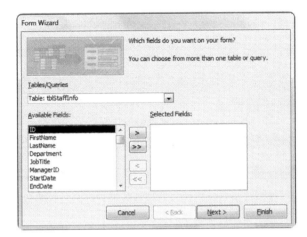

Step 2.   If the desired table or query is not selected in the **Tables/Queries** drop down box, choose the table or query you wish to work with.

Step 3.   From the list of **Available Fields,** choose the fields you want to be displayed on the form. To add a single field, select the field and use the **Add** button (**>**). To add all fields, use the **Add all** button (**>>**). When done, choose **Next**.

The **Remove** button (**<**) and the **Remove all** button (**<<**) are used to remove a selected field or all fields, respectively, from the list of selected fields.

In each of the wizard dialog boxes, the **Back** button will let you step backwards and correct previous choices.

The second dialog box of the **Form Wizard** will appear similar to the following:

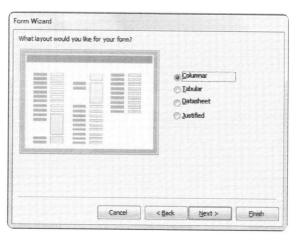

Step 4. Choose the layout style for your form. As you make a choice the preview area will indicate the form layout. The following table outlines the options. Choose one of the options and then choose **Next**.

Option	Description
Columnar	Fields are stacked vertically with labels to the left. If necessary, the Wizard will continue formatting columns of fields and labels in a left-to-right order. Only one record at a time will display.
Tabular	Fields are arranged in columns but each row resolves to a single record. The name of each field is displayed above the fields in a header area. Multiple records are displayed simultaneously.
Datasheet	The form basically mimics the **Datasheet** view of the underlying table or query. You cannot place controls on a form in **Datasheet** view, nor can you display a form's header or footer area. Multiple records are displayed.
Justified	Similar to the **Columnar** option but fields are arranged across the field in a left to right manner, from the top of the form to the bottom. Individual field labels are displayed above each field and the lengths of fields is altered to create a flush left, flush right justification. Only one record at a time will display.

The final dialog box of the **Form Wizard** will appear similar to the following:

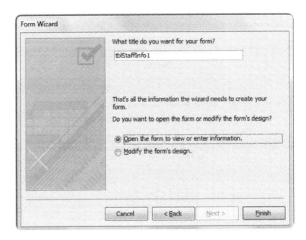

Step 5.   Type a name for the new form in the text box.

Step 6.   Choose whether to open the form in **Form View** or to modify the form's design (opened in **Form Design View**).

Step 7.   Choose **Finish**. A simple columnar form would appear similar to the following:

It is a best practice to name the form meaningfully and not accept the default name provided by the **Form Wizard**. For example, if your new form is used to view staff information you may consider using the name *frmStaffInformation* The *frm* prefix will always remind you and any future developers that the object is a form. *StaffInformation* informs one of the underlying dataset and purpose of the form.

An annoying feature of the **Form Wizard** is that it titles a form using the form name. This can be changed and the procedure is discussed when dealing with label controls in Chapter 5.

Forms and One-to-Many Joins

The **Form Wizard** makes creating forms that display data from related tables relatively easy. You have a choice between viewing data from the *many* side of a join in a *subform* or on a *linked* (pop-up) *form*. In the following examples we'll model data from the *Staff and Projects* database associated with this series. The one-to-many relationship discussed below is between the **tblStaffInfo** table and the **tblStaffSkills** table (joined one-to-many, respectively). The two tables as viewed in the **Relationship Window** appear below:

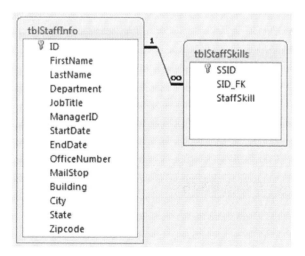

An example of a form which contains a subform is illustrated below. The subform displays those staff skill records related to the main form's current record. In this case, the staff skills of an employee named *Tonya Green*. Note that the innermost record navigator steps through the subform's records while the outermost record navigator steps through the main form's records.

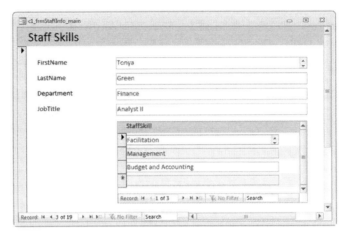

The other approach for working with related data is to use a *linked form* (these are also referred to as *pop-up forms*). An example of a linked form is illustrated below. The employees form contains a button labeled **View Skills**. When selected, the Staff Skills subform appears and displays those language records related to the main form's current record.

The following illustration is the linked subform which appears when the **View Skills** button is selected on the form in the previous illustration.

Points on Creating a Form to Display One-to-Many Related Data

- Before using the **Form Wizard**, it is important that the required relational joins be established in the **Relationship Window**.

- Although the form can be bound to a query that supplies data from two related tables, this is not necessary. You can select fields from two related tables using the Wizard. The Wizard will pull the necessary information from the **Relationship Window**.

- The form can display the data from the *many* side of the join either as a subform or as a linked form (as illustrated in the previous examples). The general design rule is to use a subform if space on the main form permits and if there is an immediate need to view the related records. Use a linked form if space is at a premium or if there is only occasional need to view the related records. You can also organize data on a form using **Tabs**, which are discussed in Chapter 6.

- When using a form which contains a subform, there will be two sets of **Record Navigator** controls. The outermost set controls movement of the records on the main form (the *one* side of the join) while the inner set controls movement through the subform records (the *many* side of the join).

- When using a form that calls a linked form to display the related records, the linked form maintains synchronization with the main form. As you move between records on the main form (the *one* side of the join), the records in the linked form will update to display the related records (the *many* side of the join).

- You do not need to include the primary or foreign key fields when designing forms in order for the related records to be synchronized. If the forms will be used to enter new records, however, the primary key must be present (unless it is an AutoNumber field) so its value can be entered. The foreign key in the subform or linked form will automatically be updated, regardless of whether it is present on the form.

How to Create a Form to Display One-to-Many Related Data

Step 1.   From the **Forms** group on the **Create** tab, choose **Form Wizard**. The first dialog box of the **Form Wizard** will appear similar to the following:

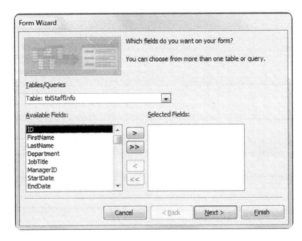

Step 2.   Start with the table on the *one* side of the join. If it is not selected in the **Tables/Queries** drop down box, choose it.

Step 3.   From the list of **Available Fields,** choose the fields from the table on the *one* side of the join that you want to be displayed on the form. To add a single field, select the field and use the **Add** button (>). To add all fields, use the **Add all** button (>>).

Step 4.   Return to the **Tables/Queries** drop down box and choose the table from the *many* side of the join.

Step 5.   Choose the field or fields from the second table, representing the *many* side of the one-to-many relationship. Ultimately, these will be displayed either in a *subform* or on a *linked form*. When finished selecting fields, choose **Next**. The second dialog box of the **Form Wizard** will appear similar to the following:

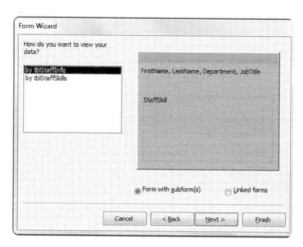

Step 6.   Select the format for the presentation of the related data by selecting either **Form with subform(s)** or **Linked forms**. Choose **Next**.

 The preview area should graphically acknowledge your intent by illustrating fields from the *one* side on the image of the main form and fields from the *many* side of the join on the subform or linked form. If the preview is incorrect, select another table in the **How do you want to view your data?** list box.

 If by choosing each of the listed tables the wizard fails to show the appropriate display of one-to-many records you may have either (1) selected an inappropriate table in Steps 2 or 4, or (2) the relationship between the tables may not be established correctly.

If you choose **Form with subform(s)** in the previous Step, a dialog box similar to the following will appear:

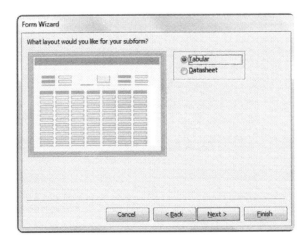

Step 7. Select **Tabular** to view columns of fields or **Datasheet** to view the subform data in a datasheet. Choose **Next** when done. The last dialog box of the **Form Wizard** will appear similar to the following.

Step 8. Type a name for the form and subform. Choose **Finish.**

See the note on page 15 concerning best practices for naming forms.

Forms and Many-to-Many Joins

Many-to-many joins actually involve three tables. An intermediary table, referred to as a *join* or a *bridge* table, is required by all relational database system to effect this join type. The bridge table at a minimum contains the foreign key fields from the other tables. Each foreign key that maps to either of the other tables is on the many side of a one-to-many join. From the perspective of the bridge table it is connected to two tables, each connection being a one-to-many join with the bridge table hosting the *many* side of each connection. In this manner the two outlying tables are connected to effect a *many-to-many* join.

The illustration below provides an example of such a join. Staff and Projects are related in a many-to-many join modeling the fact that each staff member may be assigned to zero to many projects and each project may have zero to many staff. The bridge table (here named **tblStaffandProjects**) effectively manages the specific facts about each staff:project assignment. Note that the bridge also models additional facts about a staff:project assignment, namely when the assignment was made, notes about that assignment, and the budget granted to the staff member for the specific project.

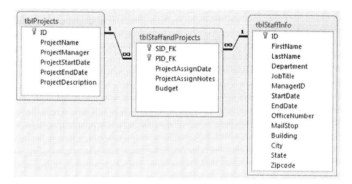

It is possible to create a form that displays data from tables joined in a many-to-many relationship using the **Form Wizard**. An issue, however, is whether to include fields from the *bridge table*.

The following illustration shows a form and subform which bridge tables in a many-to-many join. The main form displays data about *Projects* while the subform displays information about the *Staff* assigned to that project. The contents of the bridge table which connects the *Projects* and the *Staff* tables are not included in this example. This means that the form does not display such facts as when the staff:project assignment (*ProjectAssignDate*) was made, any notes about that assignment (*ProjectAssignNotes*) and the budget granted to the staff member for that project (*Budget*).

Points on Creating a Form to Display Many-to-Many Related Data

- It is not necessary to include the primary and/or foreign key fields from any of the tables provided that the intended use of the form is for viewing or editing existing data. In this configuration however, you cannot add new records.

- If you do not include foreign key fields from the bridge table, you can edit existing records on either side of the join but you cannot enter new records on either side of the join.

- Including the foreign key fields (which match the primary key fields from *both* tables) permits you to enter new records from either side of the join. However you will need to manually enter the appropriate primary and foreign key values in the appropriate fields. Creating a new record in any table will still be contingent upon the presence of validation rules, required fields, etc.

  The topic of creating a data entry form for a *many-to-many* relationship is discussed on page 174.

How to Create a Form to Display Many-to-Many Related Data

This procedure is fundamentally similar to that for creating a form to display one-to-many related data.

Step 1.   From the **Forms** group on the **Create** tab, choose **Form Wizard**. The first dialog of the **Form Wizard** will appear as illustrated on Page 18.

Step 2.	Begin by selecting the table or query that represents data on one of the members participating in the *many-to-many* join. This table or query, first selected, will appear in the main section of the form. In the example above, because the focus is on *projects* and their *staffing*, the *Projects* table and its fields are selected during this step.
Step 3.	While still viewing the first dialog box of the **Form Wizard**, select the other table from the *many* side of the join and add the appropriate fields. In the example illustrated above, the *Staffing* table is chosen in this step as the major focus is on *Projects* and then on the *Staffing* for a project.
Step 4.	Select any fields from the second table you wish to include in the subform or on the linked form.
Step 5.	While still viewing the first dialog box of the **Form** Wizard, and if desired, select the bridge table and add the foreign key fields. Review the issues outlined on the previous page if necessary.
Step 6.	Proceed with the remaining dialog boxes of the **Form Wizard** as usual.

Unbound Forms

The fundamental difference between bound and unbound forms is that an unbound form is not connected to a record source. It is not capable of displaying data from any of the database's tables or queries.

Creating an unbound form is always done in **Form Design View** as the Form Wizard requires that a record source be selected.

Since by default a form is designed to be bound to a record source, forms automatically inherit data-aware components such as the navigation and record selector controls. When creating an unbound form, which is generally used for menus and dialog boxes, you'll want to deactivate several components of a standard form. The components of interest, and how to tailor an unbound form, will be discussed in more detail in Chapter 8.

Points on Unbound Forms

- Unbound forms will not have a list of available fields related to a record source since they lack a record source.

- Unbound forms may only contain unbound controls. The exception is if you create a control bound to a *domain aggregate function*. In this case, the function may supply data from a table or query. This approach is rarely used in form design.

- Although you cannot use a wizard to create an unbound form, many of the **Control Wizards** are available when working in **Form Design View**. Like **Form Wizards**, the **Control**

Wizards are quite useful and can add important functionality to your unbound form. **Control Wizards** are discussed in Chapter 6.

How to Create an Unbound Form

Step 1.   In the **Forms** group of the **Create** tab, choose **Form Design.**

 A blank, unbound form will appear in **Form Design View**. Working with this view is the subject of the next lesson.

Step 2.   Modify the form design, if desired. The specifics of creating several types of unbound forms are discussed in Chapter 8.

Step 3.   Save the form design by selecting the **Save** button on the **Quick Access Toolbar**.

Chapter 3 | Form Design View

The **Form Design View** is used to create forms manually or to modify existing forms. When this view is available, several tabs, grouped under **Form Design Tools** may be used to manipulate form properties, adjust form and control formatting, add controls, or evoke one of several **Control Wizards**.

Several windows may be available when working in **Form Design View**. In addition to **Form Design View** window itself, which contains the current form, there are windows to adjust both form and control properties, list available fields, control tab order, or display Visual Basic for Applications (VBA) code.

Form Design vs. Form Layout Views

The more recent versions of Microsoft Access have included an additional view when working with Forms and Reports: **Form Layout** and **Report Layout** view. These views differ from the standard **Form Design** and **Report Design** view in that they permit you to view "live" data (that is to say that the form or report display the data they are bound to) while making some formatting changes. For example, the placement of controls may be adjusted and nearly any general formatting property such as font, background color, or boarder style, may be adjusted while in this view. While working in the more feature-rich **Form Design** view however, you work with the form and its controls while they are disconnected from the data source (if you are working with a bound form).

These views are certainly useful - especially when attempting to quickly create a working form or a formatted report. The **Layout** views however are relatively restrictive in some important aspects. For example, the ability to highlight a group of controls and set a group size or alignment is not available. While in **Layout** view you cannot add additional controls such as charts, lines, or grouping boxes.

Because **Layout** view has restrictions on important design activities and all of these features are available through the standard **Form Design** view, this book will focus on the more powerful design mode and allow the reader to explore the limited subset of design tools available through **Form Layout** view. It may initially seem like a limitation that you can't design a form and see the data displayed on the form at the same time, but the far richer set of controls, properties, and design tools available through the design view makes up for the deficiency of seeing data in real time.

Tabs Associated with Form Design View

The following tables outline the three tabs available when working in **Form Design View**.

Design Tab

Group	Description
Views	Switch between Form, Layout, Design, PivotTable, and PivotChart views (the latter 2 must be enabled using the Form Properties control).
Themes	Select predefined or custom themes, color groups, and/or font groups. These options are discussed in more detail later in this chapter.
Controls	Displays a palette of bound and unbound controls which may be placed on a form. Also add additional ActiveX controls. Controls are discussed in detail in Chapters 5 and 6.
Header/Footer	Add a title, logo, or a date/time text box to a form.
Tools	Manages the visibility of the properties, field list, and tab order windows. Opens a subform in a separate window, and opens the VBA code editor.

Arrange Tab

Name	Description
Table	Tools for working with table layouts, which cluster controls on a form. **Table Layouts** may be applied and removed. They are added by default to forms created using the **Form** control in the **Create** group. Table layouts are not created by default when a form is created using the **Form Wizard** or when building a form from scratch.
Rows & Columns	Tools for modifying and arranging rows and columns when working with a Table Layout. These controls are not available unless a **Table Layout** is present and selected on a form.
Merge / Split	Merges or splits controls within a **Table Layout**. Not available unless a **Table Layout** is present and selected.
Move	Moves the selected control or controls within the detail area of the form or between the detail area and the form header and footer. Only available when working with controls contained within a **Table Layout**.
Position	Sets margins, padding, and anchoring for controls contained within a **Table Layout**.
Sizing & Ordering	Sets various sizing, positioning, alignment, and *Z-order* (front/back) placements for one or more controls. These powerful controls are discussed in detail in Chapter 5.

Format Tab

Name	Description
Selection	Choose a specific control or all controls on the form (there are also methods available using the mouse and keyboard to select one or more controls - see Chapter 5).
Font	Set font attributes, and text alignment for text-based controls. The **Format Painter** is also available which permits quick copy of a broad array of formatting attributes between controls.
Number	Apply predefined format attributes to numeric, currency, and date-based fields.
Background	Apply a background graphic or set alternating row colors (if the form is set to display continuous records).
Control Formatting	Apply predefined styles and shapes to certain controls (for example, command buttons and tab controls), define conditional formatting (mainly to text-based controls), and choose fill colors, control shapes, and special effects (depending upon the control type, some tools are not available).

A Tour of Form Design View

If you create a new form using the **Form Wizard** and choose to open the form in **Form Design** view, your newly created form will appear similar to the following image. . Note that all of the controls in the **Detail** section are bound to specific fields. In **Form Design** view such controls will display the name of the binding field.

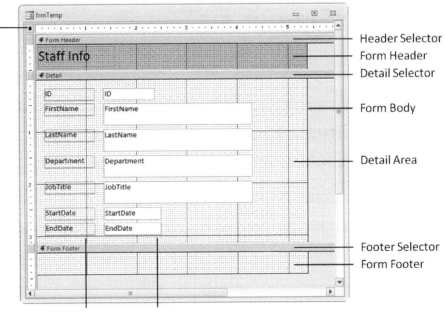

Form Selector

Header Selector

Form Header

Detail Selector

Form Body

Detail Area

Footer Selector

Form Footer

Labels   Text Boxes

Components of the Form Design View

Option	Description
Form Selector	Selects the entire form object. Double-clicking on the Form Selector will open the form's **Property Sheet**.
Header Selector	A bar that labels the header area. Single clicking on this bar selects the header. Double clicking opens the **Property Sheet** for the header.
Form Header	Contains controls which consistently appear at the top portion of the form in all views except **Form Datasheet**.
Detail Selector	A bar that labels the detail area. Single clicking on this bar selects the detail section. Double clicking opens the **Property Sheet** for the detail section.
Detail Section	Displays records from the form's record source. The controls in the detail section are generally bound to the underlying data, although the detail section may also contain unbound controls. The detail section is repeated once for each record in the form's recordset.
Form Body	A horizontal and vertical edge within the **Form Design View Window** that indicates the overall size of the form when printed or displayed on screen. If the form body is larger than the **Form Design View Window**, the form will contain **Scroll bars** when displayed on screen.
Footer Selector	A bar that labels the footer area. Single clicking on this bar selects the footer. Double clicking opens the **Property Sheet** for the footer.
Form Footer	Contains controls which consistently appear at the bottom of the form in all views except **Form Datasheet**.
Labels & Text Boxes	Data bound controls (text boxes) and their associated labels. These controls map to named fields in the form's underlying *data source*. The name of the attached field is displayed in the text box while in **Form Design** view.

The overall containing window in the illustration above is the **Form Design** window. Note the presence of rulers (top and left margin), along with scroll bars (bottom and right margin). These appear only in **Form Design** view and are not present when the form is viewed either in **Form** or **Layout** view.

Sections of a Form

Forms are complex objects. The form itself is, at a minimum, a container for the **Detail** section. In a bound form, this section is where fields in one or more records, or records from multiple tables (via subforms) are displayed. In an unbound form, the **Detail** section serves as a container for the various labels, command buttons, and other objects you wish to use.

It is not possible to remove the **Detail** section from a form, and in fact, the form as an object lacks a tangible presence. It's for this reason that to work with form properties, you first select the form by single clicking on the **Form Selector** (double clicking on it opens the **Property Sheet** for the form. Alternatively, you can choose the **Form** from the **Selection Type** drop down box on the **Property Sheet** (the **Property Sheet** is discussed in the next section).

Other sections of a form are optional and can have their visibility turned off or on. A form can display a **Form Header** and separately, a **Form Footer**. On a bound form, these areas remain constant while the user moves through the records in the **Detail** area. A form may also contain a **Page Header** and **Page Footer**. These sections are only visible when the form is viewed in **Print Preview** or when the form is printed.

Points on Form Sections

- All forms have at a minimum a detail section and the form object itself. All other sections are optional.

- The Form Header and Footer sections can contain controls that appear consistently when the form is viewed or printed. Form Headers and Footers do not appear when the form is displayed in Form Datasheet View.

- Page Header and Footer sections are only visible when the form is printed or viewed in Print Preview. These sections can contain controls which will appear at the top and bottom of each printed page. Page Headers and Footers do not appear in any other form view.

- Although the Form Header and Footer and the Page Header and Footer are paired, you can remove individual headers or footers by decreasing their height in design view to 0.

Warning: If you remove a header or footer section that contains controls, the controls will be permanently removed from the form.

How to Add Form or Page Headers and Footers

You must be in **Form Design View** to create headers and footers.

Step 1.   Right click on the **Detail** area (or the bar titled **Detail**).

Step 2.   From the short cut menu, choose **Page Header/Footer** or **Form Header/Footer,** depending upon which section you wish to display.

Repeat the procedure to remove both the **Header** and **Footer** from the desired section.

How to Remove Either a Header or a Footer using the Mouse

Headers and footers may be sized separately. To remove a header or a footer (either form or page), you adjust the size of the header or footer to zero.

Step 1.   If a **Form** or **Page Header** and **Footer** are not already present on the form, follow the previous procedure to create the desired **Header** and **Footer.**

Step 2.   Position the mouse pointer at the bottom of the **Header** or **Footer** section you wish to remove. When the mouse pointer appears as a cross with up and down-pointing arrows, drag the **Header** or **Footer** until it no longer appears

or

Step 3.   Double click on the desired **Selector** for the target header or footer (this will open the **Property Sheet** for that section).

Step 4.   From the Format tab, adjust the Header or Footer's **Height** property to 0. (Adjusting properties is discussed in the next section.)

You cannot hide a **Header** or **Footer** that contains controls. The controls must be deleted first prior to adjusting the **Header** or **Footer** height to 0.

Two Basic Approaches to Organizing Form Data

You will soon see that there are a number of form views available, both that specifically relate to the inherit design of the form or relate as the form is dynamically displaying data. Despite these numerous views most developers tend to think about forms in one of two modes.

You create **Columnar** views when you want the form to focus on one record at a time. In this view, text boxes are stacked vertically (and for large sets of fields may continue across two or more columns). The label for each text box or bound control generally appears to the left of the bound control. Forms that support basic data entry and/or editing, or the viewing of single records are best suited to this design approach.

Data arranged on a form as **Tabular** organization arrange individual fields across a single row. The attached labels appear in the form header and thus act like column headings. The form is configured to display data from multiple records, each occupying a single row. In this mode a **Tabular** format resembles that of a table (except that forms offer additional functionality such as macros, command buttons, and attaching Visual Basic for Applications code). When a developer wishes to create a form that supports quick views of data across multiple records, the **Tabular** format is the general choice.

Form Views

By default, a form may have a variety of form views applied. As discussed in the previous section, there are a number of properties that a developer can use to limit or control which views are available and how a form appears when opened. This includes how many records are displayed at a time when a form is viewed in **Form** or **Layout** view.

By default, a form has three views available: **Form**, **Layout**, and **Form Design**. There are other views which may be activated: **Datasheet**, **PivotTable**, and **PivotChart** are all properties of the form object itself. To enable these additional views you modify **Format** properties of the form (discussed in the next section).

Points on Form Views

- There are only two broad categories of form views: Form and Design. When a bound form is either in **Form, Layout, Datasheet, PivotTable**, or **PivotChart** view, the form will display data. **Design** and **Layout** view are used to modify design attributes, although as previously mentioned only **Design** view offers you full control over form design. If the form is bound, records cannot be displayed while the form is in **Form Design** view.

- You can modify the form's properties to include additional views. These being **Datasheet, PivotTable**, and **PivotChart** view. These are only available to bound forms and each view is a separate property of the form. Setting a property to *yes* enables the view while setting it to *no* disables it. When enabled the view is available from the **View** control on the **Home** tab.

- A bound form in **Form** or **Layout** view has a property, **Default View** which further refines how the form appears. The following section details these default views.

- If a form contains a Form Header and/or a Form Footer, those only appear when the form is in **Form** or **Layout** view. Headers and/or footers are out of context in **Datasheet, PivotTable**, and **PivotChart** views.

- If a form contains a Page Header and/or a Page Footer, those sections will only appear in Print Preview, or when the form is printed.

- The developer has no control over Print Preview. Access uses the form's Default View property to control how the form will appear when printed or previewed. There is no capability to print or preview the form as it appears in Form Design View.

Understanding the Default View Property

When you open a form in either **Form** or **Layout** view, a property of the form named **Default View** controls how the form appears. A few of the available settings broadly control the form view (such as **PivotTable**, and **PivotChart**). However, other values of the **Default View** property control how records are displayed within the form's **Detail** section.

As an example, consider the following form as it appears in **Form Design** view. The form is bound to a table that contains staff information. The bound text boxes (connected to the fields *FirstName, LastName, StartDate* and *EndDate* are arranged in a row in the **Detail** section. Labels for each of the controls have been placed in the **Form Header** section. The form appears as:

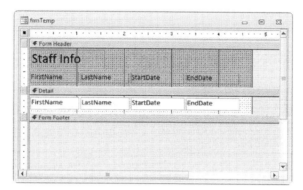

If the form's **Default View** property is set to *Single form* when viewed in **Form View** it would appear similar to the following. Note that in this view a single record is displayed at a time. The overall size of the **Form Design** window sets the height of the form in **Form View**:

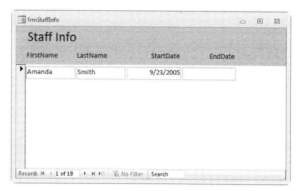

If the form's **Default View** property is set to *Continuous Forms* then when the form is opened in **Form View**, it would appear similar to the following:

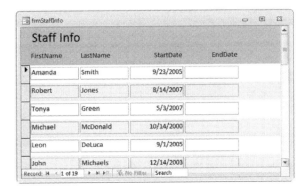

When the **Default View** has been set to *Continuous Forms* the height of each row of data is controlled by the height of the **Detail** section. The number of records visible on the form (in other words the number or rows) is a function of the height of the **Detail** section as well as the height of the **Form Design Window.**

The remaining setting for the **Default View** property is *Split Form*. In this view one section of the form displays the contents of a single record while the other portion of the form displays a **Datasheet.** The **Datasheet** synchronizes with the single record display: choosing a record from the **Datasheet** area updates the display of the single record. Note that this view is one of the quick form types available from the **More Forms** control on the **Forms** group of the **Create** tab. A split form would appear similar to the following:

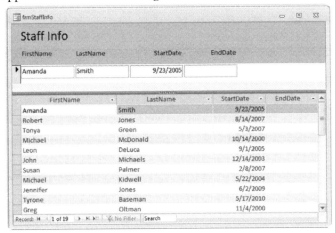

One additional value, *Datasheet*, of the **Default View** property essentially turns the form into a standard **Datasheet.** The form used in the previous examples would appear as the following in **Datasheet** view:

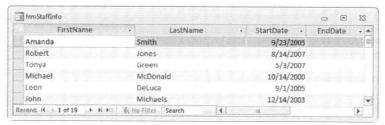

While **Datasheet** view can be useful for some situation (applied to a *subform*, for example), you lose all aspects of a form in this view. Note in the previous illustration that the form's header (*Staff info*) is lost in this view. Any controls such as command buttons and options groups would also not display.

Other Form Views

In addition to the general views discussed so far, there are some additional properties of a form that can control specific behaviors. For example, you can set properties to force the form to be used only for viewing data (thus preventing any data entry or editing). Alternatively, you can set a form so it is only used to enter new data - the ability to view existing data using the form as been removed. Lastly, for unbound forms that serve as important dialog boxes, you can adjust properties so the dialog box is either always on top of other objects in your database, or must be addressed in order to regain focus on other objects - this latter mode is termed a *modal* dialog box. The following table summarizes the properties necessary to elicit these form modes.

Common Form Behaviors

Mode	Behavior	Property Settings
General Data Entry/Data Viewing	Form opens in Form View User is free to change to Datasheet view Records can be edited, deleted, or added.	**Default View**: *Single Form, Continuous Forms, or Split Form* **Allow Form View** *Yes*
View Records Only	Form opens in Form View User cannot change views Records may only be viewed No new records may be created	**Default View**: *Single Form, Continuous Forms, or Split Form* **Allow Form View**: *Yes* **Allow Edits**: *No* **Allow Deletions**: *No* **Allow Additions**: *No*
General Data Entry: New Records Only	Form opens in Form View. User cannot change views Only new records are added User cannot view existing records. Only views supported are *Single* and *Split Form*.	**Default View**: *Single Form or Split Form* **Allow Form View**: *Yes* **Data Entry**: *Yes*
Dialog Box - Always on Top	Form rides above all other open objects in your database.	**Modal**: *No* **Pop up**: *Yes*
Dialog Box - Modal	Form floats above all other Access windows No other Access window can gain focus until form is closed User cannot resize form	**Border Style**: *Dialog* **Pop up**: *Yes* **Modal**: *Yes*

Form Properties

Forms are the most complex objects an Access database can contain. Because a bound form can be interactive (whereas a bound report is view-only), it comes with a complex suite of properties that mediate the nature of the data binding. Unbound forms have many properties as well - it's just that the properties that related to the nature of the binding between the form and the underlying data source are not relevant. The various form sections (headers, detail, and footers) also have their own attendant suite of properties, both dealing with data binding as well as general format attributes, but in this section we will focus on the various categories of properties associated with the form as an object. Recall from the illustration on page 28 that in order to select the form object you single or double click on the **Form Selector**. The double clicking action will select the form and open the **Property Sheet** associated with the form. All form properties are set by using the **Property Sheet**.

How to Change a Form Property

You should be in either **Form Layout** or **Form Design View** in order to work with the **Property Sheet**. Note that not all properties on a form may be changed while in **Form Layout View**. This procedure assumes that a form is opened in **Form Design View**.

Step 1.   Double-click on the **Form Selector**, or select the **Form Selector**, then select the **Properties** button on the **Form Design** toolbar. A property sheet similar to the following will appear:

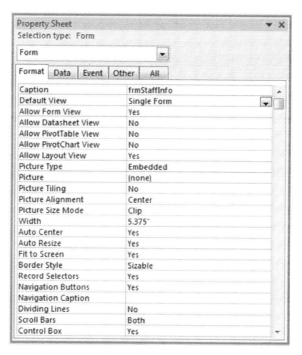

Property Sheet Category Tabs

Tab	Description
Format	Lists properties that affect the visual appearance of the form. This ranges from the type of form view permitted to the style of the form's border.
Data	Displays properties which control how the form interacts with its underlying record source and how the form will interact with the user (for example by denying the ability to edit a record). Unbound forms will have these properties, although some entries will be blank.
Event	Lists *events* the form can respond to. An event is some action, elicited by either the user or by the database. Forms or controls respond to an event either through a macro or by using VBA (Visual Basic for Applications) code.
Other	Lists properties that do not readily fall into the above-listed categories.
All	Displays all properties in a single list.

Step 2.　　Select the desired **Category Tab**.

Step 3.　　Select the text box for the desired property.

Step 4.　　Depending upon the property selected, do one of the following:

Type a new property value

Filter	Department="Finance"

Or select a new property value from the drop-down list

Recordset Type	Dynaset	▾

Or select the **Builder (...)** and use it to create a new property value.

Back Color	Background 1	▾	⋯

 Not all properties have a builder or a drop-down list.

The new property takes effect when you move to another property, select the form or a form control, or close the **Property Sheet**.

Common Form Format Properties

Option	Description
Caption	Sets the text that appears on the form's **Title bar**.
Default View	Specifies which form view is used when the form is opened. Options include *Single Form, Continuous Form, Datasheet, PivotTable, PivotChart,* and *Split Form.*
Allow Layout View	Controls whether **Form Layout View** appears as an option on the **View** control.
Picture	Specifies the name of the graphic file for the form's background image.
Picture Size Mode	Controls how the form's background image is sized on the form. Options include *Clip, Stretch,* and *Zoom.*
Auto Center	Determines whether the form always centers itself on the screen when opened.
Border Style	Controls whether the form can be resized or not by the user when open. Options include *None, Thin, Sizable,* and *Dialog.*
Scroll Bars	Specifies whether **Scroll bars** appear on a form. Note that scroll bars only appear when the form body is larger than the form window. Options include *Horizontal, Vertical, Both,* and *Neither.*
Record Selectors	Controls whether a **Record Selector** appears on the form. This is used to select the current record for delete, copy, cut, and, paste operations.
Navigation Buttons	Indicates whether a **Navigation Control** is present on the form.
Control Box	Indicates whether a **Control Box** will appear on the form. This control is a standard Windows element, located at the extreme upper left corner of most windows, and contains the **Control Menu**.
Close Button	Sets the presence or absence of the **Close** button on the form's extreme upper right.
Min Max Buttons	Sets the presence or absence of the **Minimize, Maximize** and **Restore** buttons on the form's extreme upper right corner.

 Warning: **Do not** *remove the close button and the control box without providing an alternative way to close the form!*

Common Form Data Properties

Property	Description
Record Source	Specifies the form's record source. If the record source is a table or a named query the object's name is displayed. If the record source is an SQL statement, the statement is displayed. You can evoke a **Builder** to create or modify an SQL statement for the record source.
Filter	Specifies the filter conditions for the form. Generally a form does not have a filter unless it is based on a table or query that has a saved filter. When a user creates and saves a filter this property is automatically updated.
Order by	Controls how the recordset data are ordered. If a user sorts a form and saves the sort order, this property is automatically updated.
Data Entry	Specifies whether the form opens displaying records or opens to a blank, new record. The default, *No*, indicates that the form opens and displays existing records. Note that in the default mode, the form is capable of accepting new records as long as **Allow Additions** is set to *Yes*.
Allow Additions	Specifies whether the user can add new records. The default value is *Yes*.
Allow Deletions	Controls whether records can be deleted. The default value is *Yes*.
Allow Filters	Controls whether the user can apply filters to the form.
Allow Edits	Specifies whether the user can make changes to saved records. The default value is *Yes*.
Allow Filters	Specifies whether filters can be applied to the form when it is open in **Form View**. If set to *No*, some controls in the **Filter & Group** group are disabled.

Common Form Events

Event	Description
On Current	Occurs when the form displays the first record in a recordset, and fires every time the form is moved to another record.
Before Update	Triggered when the form senses a change in a recordset, but before the change is committed to the recordset.
After Update	Triggered after a change is committed to the recordset.
On Delete	Occurs when the user acts to delete a record, but before the record is actually deleted.
On Dirty	Fires when any bound control on a form changes value due to an edit by the end user.
On Open	Triggered when the form is opened, but immediately before any records are displayed.
On Close	Triggered when the form is closed, and removed from the screen.

Event processing requires a macro or Visual Basic for Applications (VBA) code. The property's text box displays either the name of a macro or the term *Event Procedure* depending upon whether a macro or a VBA procedure is attached, respectively.

There are over 50 individual events associated with the form object. Events are important entry points into the world of VBA programming. There is a title in this series, *Building VBA Applications Using Microsoft Access* which covers event processing in greater detail.

Common Other Form Properties

Property	Description
Pop Up	Specifies whether the form behaves as a *pop up* form, in which case the form always floats above other windows. If used in conjunction with the **Modal** and **Border Style** properties, you can create custom dialog boxes. The default is *No*.
Modal	Controls whether the form must be closed before you can activate other windows in Access. The default is *No*.
Cycle	Sets the behavior of how the form responds to the *Tab* key. The options are *All Records* (use *Tab* to move from the last control on one record to the first control on the next record), *Current Record* (*Tab* moves from the last control on the current record to the first control on the same record) or *Current Page* (if the form is multi-page, *Tab* moves to the first control on the next page of the form).
Ribbon Bar	Specifies a custom Ribbon Bar to be displayed when the form is opened in **Form** or **Layout View**.

Themes, Colors and Fonts

Microsoft has replaced the *auto layout* feature in previous versions of Access with the more broadly applicable concept of *themes*. A theme is a predefined set of color and font attributes that is available to most members of the Microsoft Office suite (such as Access, Word, Excel, and PowerPoint). Themes, as named collections of style elements, are the same across the Office Suite family so you can coordinate the same look and feel in your work environment.

In Access, themes can be used to quickly format forms and reports. For forms, a theme specifies the background color, and font attributes for form sections and their controls.

You can apply a theme to a single form or report, to several forms or reports, or to all objects in the current database. When a theme is applied to a form, individual format properties of the affected elements and controls are modified *en masse*. If you override a theme color for one or more controls or sections on a form that has an applied theme and you choose a non-theme color you break those sections and/or controls from the theme settings. Applying a new theme to the form will not affect the sections or controls with the manually applied, non-theme colors. This rule applies to background colors and fonts as well. For these reasons take care when applying a theme to one or more objects in your database if your intent is to further modify some attributes that participate in themes.

How to Apply or Change a Theme

You must be in either **Form Layout** or **Form Design View** to apply a theme. If a theme has already been applied to the database, all forms and/or reports, or the current object, this project may be used to change the theme settings for the entire database, all forms or reports, or the current object.

Step 1.   On the **Design** tab, in the **Themes** group, choose **Themes**. A drop down panel similar to the following will appear:

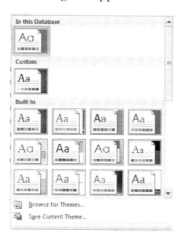

Theme Options

Option	Description
In this Database	Displays the current theme for the database, as well as any themes that have been applied to individual forms or reports.
Custom	Lists any custom themes installed on the local computer.
Built-In	Shows a gallery of 40 built-in Microsoft Office themes.
Browse for Themes…	Look for themes installed on the local machine or on your network.
Save Current Theme…	Save the current theme.

Step 2.   Move the mouse pointer over any theme displayed within the list of themes. As the mouse moves over a theme the form and it's controls will update to show the current theme's design attributes.

Step 3.   Left-click on the desired theme to apply it to all database objects, or right-click and select from the following options:

Option	Description
Apply Theme to All Matching Objects	If the current object is a form, applies the theme to all forms. If the current object is a report, applies the theme to all reports.
Apply Theme to This Object Only	Applies the theme only to the current form or report.
Make This Theme the Database Default	Applies the theme to all database objects. This is the same as left-clicking on the named theme.
Delete	Deletes the current theme (only available for custom themes).
Add Gallery to Quick Access Toolbar	Places a reference to the **Theme Gallery** in the **Quick Access** toolbar.

How to Create a Custom Theme

When you create a custom theme you first set design attributes for a form or report, and while either in **Layout** or **Design View** you save the theme. Themes are saved as files using the *.thmx* file extension, generally in a path that terminates in Appdata\Microsoft\Templates\Document Themes. If you need to determine the exact location of themes on your computer you may wish to search on files with the *.thmx* extension.

Step 1.   Select an existing form, or create a new form and open it in **Form Design** or **Form Layout View**.

Step 2.   Apply background, foreground colors and fills as desired to form sections, and controls that accept these attributes.

Step 3.   Apply font name, font size, and font colors to controls that accept these attributes.

Step 4.   From the **Design** tab, in the **Themes** group, select the **Themes** drop down box.

Step 5.   Select **Save Current Theme...**

Step 6.   Provide a name for your theme and choose **Save**.

 A best practice is to accept the default location for your custom theme. This will make it available to all theme galleries in all Microsoft Office applications that work with themes.

Table Layout

Table Layout is a design and control arrangement tool that is new to Access 2010. Conceptually it acts like a table you may have worked with in Microsoft Word, where rows or columns contain controls and their associated labels (depending upon the initial orientation that is applied or that you choose). This layout applies both to forms and reports and is automatically added to a form or report that is created using the **Form** or **Blank Form** controls located in the **Forms** group (for reports, use the similarly-named controls in the **Reports** group). For forms, the **Table Layout** is also added for forms created using **Multiple Items** or **Split Form** options available from the **More Forms** control located within the **Forms** group. You can also add **Table Layout** to any existing form by simply selecting two or more controls on the form and choosing a desired layout from the **Arrange** tab. A form or report may contain multiple **Table Layouts**.

There are two basic grids: **Stacked** and **Tabular** (these are similar to the Columnar and Tabular layouts offered when you use the **Form Wizard** - discussed on page 13). Stacked layout arranges labels and their associated controls on rows: labels in the left-hand column and controls arranged in the right column. Each label-control pair initially occupies a separate row in the table. The **Tabular** layout places controls in a row within the form's **Detail** section and the attached labels appear in the **Form Header** area. Each table row may contain multiple controls (in the detail portion) and multiple, associated labels in the form header section.

Points on Table Layout

- Regardless of how **Table Layout** is applied, you work with a table-like grid, only visible in **Form Layout** or **Form Design View**, that serves to arrange and contain the controls, labels, and other objects placed within the layout area.

- In layout or design mode the grid behaves dynamically. You can move controls or objects around within the grid and it responds by creating new rows or columns, depending upon your mouse actions.

- Within a given column all controls must occupy the same width. For a given row, all controls must maintain the same height. To create individual controls that are wider or higher than their neighbors, you must add additional columns or rows and merge the desired cells to create the excess width or height that you need.

- Think of the **Table Layout** as a quick-format tool for form or report design. When you work with forms or reports that don't contain a **Table Layout** you lose the quick formatting this controls offers but gain more flexibility to move and arrange controls individually.

A **Table Layout**, viewed in **Form Layout** view, appears in the following illustration. Note the **Table Selector** element in the upper right hand corner of the table. This control serves to select and/or move the **Table Layout** control in a manner similar to selecting and moving tables in Microsoft Word.

ID	8
FirstName	Amanda
LastName	Smith
Department	Finance
JobTitle	Director

How to Add a Table Layout

A **Table Layout** is automatically added if you create a form using the **Form, Blank Form, Multiple Items**, or **Split Form** controls from within the **Form** group on the **Create** tab. You add a **Table Layout** whenever you create a form using the **Form Wizard**, via the **Form Design** control (**Form** group), or if you need an additional layout for a form. **Table Layout** and its associated tools are only available in **Form Design** or **Form Layout** view.

When manually adding a **Table Layout** you must select one or more controls on the form first. It is not possible to add a blank **Table Layout** - they always contain one or more controls.

Step 1.   Select one or more controls on your form. Selecting controls is discussed on page 65.

Step 2.   From the **Arrange** tab, in the **Table** group, choose **Stacked** or **Tabular**.

How to Remove a Table Layout

This procedure only removes the **Table Layout** structure. The controls it contained remain on the form.

Step 1.   Select any control within the desired **Table Layout**.

Step 2.   From the **Table** group on the **Arrange** tab, select **Remove Layout**.

You can also right-click within the **Table Layout** and choose **Layout, Remove Layout** from the short cut menu.

How to Arrange Items in Table Layout

Once a **Table Layout** exists, you can move controls, add or delete rows or columns, and merge or split cells. The majority of these actions can be mediated either by using the **Table** group controls, or right-clicking within a table and choosing the desired action from the short cut menu.

Step 1.　　Position the insertion point at the desired location within the **Table Layout**. Use the following table as a guide to available actions.

Action	Procedure
Move a Control	Select the control and drag it to the desired location. Note that if you only select the label or text box from a label/text box pair only the selected item will move. To move a control and it's label, select both items first.
Add a Row or Column	These commands are available from the **Table** group, **Arrange** tab, or via the short cut menu. **Insert Above** adds a new row above the insertion point. **Insert Below** adds a new row below the insertion point. **Insert Left** adds a column to the left of the insertion point. **Insert Right** adds a column to the right of the insertion point.
Delete a Row or Column	These commands are only available by right clicking and choosing from the short cut menu. **Delete Row** removes the current row - all controls within the row are also deleted. **Delete Column** removes the current column. Any controls are also removed.
Split a Cell	Select the desired cell. Choose either **Split Vertically** or **Split Horizontally**.
Merge Split Cells	This procedure only merges empty cells, or a pair of cells with one cell empty. Select the cells to merge. Choose **Merge**.

Any of the above-listed actions can be undone if necessary. Press *Ctrl Z* or from the **Quick Access** toolbar, choose **Undo**.

Chapter 4 | Data-Bound Forms

A *bound* form is connected to a *record source* such as a table or query and is therefore suited to display data for entering, editing or analysis. *Bound* forms typically contain *controls* that are also *bound*. *Bound controls* are connected to a field from the form's record source and are used to display, edit, or enter data. Bound forms nearly always make up the majority of the form type found in a database application.

Points on Bound Forms

- When you create a form that is based on a single table, the form is *bound* only to that table. The table is referred to as the form's *record source*.

- Forms that display data from two or more tables related in a one-to-many join generally use *subforms* to display the related data. The *main form* will use the table from the *one* side of the join as its record source while the *subform* uses the table from the *many* side of the join. Specific form properties link the form and subform together using the primary and foreign keys.

- When working with forms that display data from two or more tables related in a *many-to-many* join, the *main form* will use one of the tables as its record source (this depends upon which table was initially chosen using a wizard) while the subform displaying records from the other table will utilize an SQL statement as its record source. **Form Wizards** build these SQL statements automatically and they join the *bridge table* and the other table from the *many-to-many* join. Specific form properties link the form and subform together using the primary and foreign keys. The Wizard's task is made easier if the joins between all tables have previously been established in the **Relationships Window.**

- Regardless of the nature of the record source, all the fields in the record source are available to the form via the **Field List** which is available in both **Form Design** and **Form Layout** views.

- *Bound* forms can contain both *bound* and *unbound* controls. In addition, there are a number of **Control Wizards** that make working with controls easier.

- If the record source (table or query) for a form is modified that behavior may affect the form. Deleting a field in a record source will disconnect any controls which were bound to it. On the form they will display the error state **#Name?** while renaming a field under most conditions will not affect the bound control (although its associated label value may change). Adding an additional field will not affect the form - rather, the new field will appear in the form's **Field List.**

SQL (Structured Query Language - the letters are spelled out) is a query definition language used by Access and all major database systems. All Access queries are converted into SQL statements before the query is run.

The Form as a Data-Bound Object

A form bound to a record source is a sophisticated object that manages many functions. When a bound form is opened it automatically connects to its record source, and also manages link and update operations for each of its bound controls. Generally, bound forms contain a *record navigator* so the user can step forward or backward through the bound records. During each step to another record, the form manages the linkage between its controls and the underlying recordset to constantly update the bound controls. If the form is set to permit data entry and/or editing and deleting of data, then changes or deletes to existing data are also mediated by the form. Lastly, if a form contains one or more *subforms*, in order to display data from related tables, the containing (or *parent*) form also manages synchronization between itself and its one or more subforms.

Much of these interactions go unnoticed by the end user or the casual form designer. As will be discussed, there are some properties of the form that can be adjusted to control how some interactions between the form and its record source are realized. Although beyond the scope of this book, the real power of a bound form exists in the *events* that are triggered when a form is opened, connects to a record source, synchronizes bound controls, steps through records, mediates additions, edits and/or deletions to data, and then disconnects from its record source and closes. These events (there are 50!) provide the developer with detailed control over how a form behaves.

We'll touch some on VBA (Visual Basic for Applications) programming in this book. A far more detailed discussion of this topic may be found in the title *Building VBA Applications Using Microsoft Access 2010* which is part of this series.

Bound Forms and Bound Controls

If a bound form is in **Form Design** or **Form Layout** view, you can review the list of available fields by displaying the **Field List**. Any field dragged from this list onto the form becomes a *bound control*. Although the most common control type is a **Text Box**, Access determines the type of control based upon the field's data type. For example, inserting a field of the *Yes/No* data type will typically create a **Check Box** control while inserting a field of the *OLE Object* data type will insert a **Bound Object Frame** control. If a field on a table is associated with a *lookup* then Access will add a **Combo Box**.

Controls that can display text will show the name of the bound field when viewed in **Form Design View**. An example of a set of text boxes bound to fields (FirstName, LastName, and

Department) is illustrated below. Note that the labels associated with each **Text Box** inherit the field name as their display property.

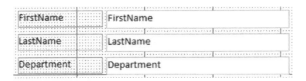

Properties Controlling Bound Forms and Controls

Object	Properties
Form	The **record source** property names the table or query or displays the *SQL Statement* that is used to provide the records for the form.
Control	The **control source** property lists the field from the form's **Record Source** to which the control is bound.
Subform	**Source object** names the form contained by the **Subform** control.
	The **Link master fields** property lists the fields which constitute the primary key in the relationship join.
	Link child fields property lists the foreign key fields in the relationship join.

How to View the Field List

The field list is only available when the form is in **Form Layout** or **Form Design** view.

Step 1.   From the **Tools** group of the **Design** tab, choose **Add Existing Fields**. The **Field List** will appear similar to the following illustration.

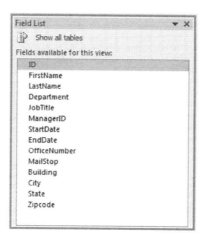

Step 2.   If you wish to view additional tables, select the **Show all tables** hyperlink. The **Field List** will appear similar to the following:

Field List Options

Option	Description
Fields available for this view	Displays the fields associated with the form's current *record source* property.
Fields available in related tables	Displays all tables related to the form's current *record source*. The tables that appear in this area are derived from the tables defined in the **Relationships Window**.
Fields available in other tables	Shows all other tables from the current database. Unless you can manually show Access that a table in this area is related to the form's current *record source* Access will not permit fields to be added to the current form.

How to Modify a Form's Record Source

Use this procedure to change the table, query, or SQL statement that specifies the form's record source. This procedure would generally be conducted if you need to add additional fields to the record source.

Step 1.　Open the **Property Sheet** by double-clicking on the **Form Selector**, or if the **Property Sheet** is open, ensure that it is displaying properties for the form by single-clicking on the **Form Selector**.

Step 2.　On the **Property Sheet**, select the **Data** tab.

Step 3.　Select the text box that corresponds to the **Record Source** property.

Step 4.　If you wish to change the **Record Source** to an existing table or query, select the new **Record Source** from the drop-down list. This action would end the procedure. Alternatively, to modify an existing SQL statement or to create a new SQL statement, select the **Builder (...)**.

Step 5.　If the **Record Source** was formerly a table, you will be prompted as to whether you wish to create a query based on the table. Choose **Yes** to continue or **No** to cancel this process. If you chose **Yes**, the **Query Builder** will appear.

Step 6.　In the **Query Builder**, add or remove fields and/or tables as desired.

Step 7.　Close the **Query Builder** when done. A dialog box similar to the following will appear:

Step 8. Choose **Yes** to save the query as an SQL statement for the form's **Record Source** property, or choose **No** to abandon changes to the form's **Record Source** property, or choose **Cancel** to return to the **Query Builder**.

If you save the query from within the **Query Builder**, it becomes a named query and will appear in the list of queries in the **Database Window**.

SQL statements generated by the **Query Builder** may contain *criteria expressions* and specify *sort orders*.

How to Add a Field to a Form

When you add a field to a form Access determines the control type based on the data type of the field. Most data types resolve to a **Text Box** whereas the yes/no data type will result in a **Checkbox** and an OLE database will map to a **Bound Object Frame**. Once placed, you can change the control type if required. This procedure is discussed on page 80.

Step 1. Ensure that the desired field is visible from the **Field List**. You may need to scroll the list to view the field.

Step 2. Use the mouse to drag the field to the desired section of the form and release the mouse when done.

Step 3. Adjust the control's position, size, and design properties as desired. These adjustments are discussed in Chapter 5.

The following table outlines the type of bound control that will be placed on a form depending upon the underlying data type of the desired field.

Control/Data Type Associations

Field Data Type	Control
Text	Text box.
Memo	Text box.
Number	Text box.
Date/Time	Text box with date picker enabled.
Currency	Text box with *currency* format set.
Autonumber	Text box.
Yes/No	Check box.
OLE Object	Bound Object Frame.
Hyperlink	Text box.
Attachment	Attachment.
Calculated	Text box.
Lookup	Combo Box.

You can drag several fields from the **Field List** at once. To select multiple contiguous fields, hold down the *Shift* key while selecting the fields. To select multiple, non-contiguous fields, hold down the *Ctrl* key while selecting fields. When done, drag any selected field onto the form and release.

How to Delete a Bound Control

You must be in **Form Layout** or **Form Design** view to delete a control.

Step 1. Select the desired control by clicking once on it. The control will become highlighted.

Step 2. Press the *Delete* **key.**

When you select a control that has an attached label, this action deletes both objects. If you wish to only delete the attached label, select only the label by clicking on it, then press *Delete*.

How to Change a Bound Control's Control Source Property

By changing the **Control Source** property you change the field to which the control is bound.

Step 1.   Select the desired control.

Step 2.   Display the **Property Sheet** if necessary.

Step 3.   On the **Property Sheet**, select the **Data** tab.

Step 4.   Select the text box associated with the **Control Source** property.

Step 5.   Select another field from the drop-down list.

The **Control Source** drop down box displays all fields associated with the parent form's **Record Source**.

How to Save a Form Design

Whenever you modify the design of a form and attempt to close any of the form views, you will be prompted to save changes to the form design. You may save the form design at that point or follow this procedure to save the form as you desire.

Step 1.   From the **Quick Access** toolbar, select the **Save** button.

Chapter 5 | Form Controls

Overview of Form Controls

Controls serve two broad tasks on a form. Bound controls display field data from the form's underlying record source. Unbound controls provide additional functionality to the form such as explanatory labels and command buttons that evoke functional tasks.

If you use one of the **Form Wizards** to create a form, the wizard will create bound and unbound controls. The bound controls will display the field values you requested when you defined the form. The unbound controls are labels and, depending upon the style you choose, the Wizard may include line controls as a style element. **Form Wizards** do not add command buttons, option frames, or other sophisticated controls, and in Chapter 6 we'll tour these controls in more detail.

When creating a form manually, or when modifying the design of a form created by a **Form Wizard**, you add controls either by dragging fields from the **Field List** or by selecting the appropriate control from the **Control Toolbox** and drawing the control on the form.

Controls, like forms, have properties that specify or set important formatting, data, and usability attributes. The **Property Sheet** will display the properties for the currently selected control on a form. For controls that display text, such as labels and text boxes, you can also adjust formatting properties by using the **Formatting** tab.

Bound and Unbound Controls

Generally, bound controls are created by dragging fields from the **Field List** and unbound controls are created by working with the appropriate control tool from the **Control Toolbar**. Bound controls that display text will show the name of the field they are bound to. Similar controls that are unbound will display the text *Unbound*.

Points on Bound and Unbound Controls

- You can bind an unbound control created by using a control tool on the Control Toolbar by modifying the control's Field Source property.

- If the form's Record Source property is modified and a field is removed, the bound control for that field will display the message **#Name?** You should either delete the control or modify its Field Source property to bind it to another field.

- Combo Boxes and List Boxes are special cases of bound controls. The data they display as a list may come from a source in the database other than the field they are bound to. For example, a combo box on a form bound to a table called Employee Information might display a list of departments from a separate table which only stores department names (developers generally refer to this second table as a *lookup table*). The specific department the user selects from the Combo or List Box is then stored in a field called Department in the Employee Information table.

- A subset of the bound control is the *calculated* control. This control usually refers to one or more other bound controls in its *Control Source* property. The control is connected to the forms underlying record source but isn't itself bound. An example of this would be a text box that has the *Control Source* =[FirstName] & " " & [LastName]. If the form is bound to a record source with [FirstName] and [LastName] fields, the calculated control would display a full name (first name, space, last name) for the current record. Creating a calculated control is discussed in Chapter 7.

- The specific bound control type associated with the data type for a field is explained in the table on page 54.

Warning: Although you can unbind a bound control (you may wish to convert the control into a *calculated control*), this is **not** recommended. Access sets properties for the bound control and in most circumstances you'll need to reset these to achieve the desired formatting or behavior. When creating a calculated control it is best to start with a new unbound control of the appropriate type by using a control tool from the **Control** group.

How to Add a Bound Control from the Field List

Most fields will create a text box when dragged onto a form. Fields with some data types such as Yes/No or OLE Object will create **Check Box** or **Bound Object Frames**, respectively. Note that controls can be changed into other control types. This is discussed on page 80.

Step 1.   Ensure that the desired field is visible from the **Field List**. You may need to scroll the list to view the field.

Step 2.   Use the mouse to drag the field to the desired section of the form and release the mouse when done.

Step 3.   Adjust the control's position, size and, design properties as desired. These adjustments are discussed in Chapter 5

Naming Controls

Every control on a form has an associated **Name** property. If not manually entered, Access will sequentially number controls using the control type as part of the control name. Example: *Command41* or *Check3*. If you intend on writing expressions that refer to controls, or intend on using Visual Basic for Applications (VBA) code, it is good practice to provide meaningful names for your controls and not default to the Access naming scheme. This is important because accessing a property associated with a control, either in VBA or via an expression, takes the syntax *ControlName.Property*. The dot between the name and the property signifies that the property is an attribute of the control. Providing a meaningful name to a control means that it is easier to formulate an expression and the expressions and/or VBA code become easier to read and understand. The expression *txtDisplayTotal.value = txtSalary.value + txtBenefint.value* is far more understandable than the expression *Text41.value = Text30.value + Text107.value*

How to Name a Control

You can be in **Form Layout** or **Form Design View** for this procedure.

Step 1.   Select the desired control.

Step 2.   On the **Design** tab, in the **Tools** group, choose **Property Sheet**.

Step 3.   Move to the **Other** tab.

Step 4.   Enter a name for the control in the **Name** text area.

 Some developers go one step further and prefix a control name with an abbreviation of the control type. For example, the prefixes *txt, cmd, optfm,* and *img* would refer to a text box, command button, option frame, and image control, respectively.

The Controls Group

The **Controls** group contains a variety of controls that may be added to a form. Several controls also have **Control Wizards** associated with them. When the **Control Wizard** is enabled and you add the appropriate control type to a form, its wizard automatically starts and steps you through the process of setting specific control properties. **Control Wizards** are discussed in Chapter 6.

The **Controls** group is located on the **Form Layout Tools** or the **Form Design Tools** tab, depending upon which view you are working with. Only a subset of controls are available when in **Form Layout** view, thus to realize the full potential of this group you should be in **Form Design** view.

Components of the Control Group

Name	Button	Description
Select		Selects a control or group of controls, a section of a form, or the form itself. This is the default control in the Control group.
Label	*Aa*	Creates a label control. Labels display text and are always *unbound*. Labels are automatically associated with other controls such as text boxes.
Text Box	abl	Creates a text box. Text boxes display multiple lines of text. A text box may be bound or unbound. If the text box is bound to a field of the *Date/Time* data type, a **Date Picker** automatically appears associated with the text box.
Button	xxxx	Creates a command button. These are controls that respond when selected by firing a macro or a VBA procedure. The **Command Button Wizard** offers useful options. Buttons are always unbound.
Tab Control		Inserts a tab control onto a form. This is a multi-page control that acts much like common tabbed dialogs, such as the **Property Sheet** dialog box. Each tab may contain its own complement of controls. Tabs are always unbound.
Hyperlink		Actually a **Label** control, the **Hyperlink** inserts a reference to another object in the database, a file on your computer, or a web page. Clicking on the hyperlink text opens the appropriate application (such as a web browser) and loads the target file. This control is unbound.
Web Browser		Creates a small web browser than can be embedded on the form. This control may be bound or unbound.
Navigation		Inserts a **Navigation Control**, which consists of one or more **Navigation Buttons** and a **Navigation Subform**. Navigation controls allow you to create forms that permit easy switching between other forms and reports. This control is only unbound.
Option Group	XYZ	Creates a group of option buttons, check boxes, or toggle buttons. In a frame, only one control may be selected at a time. Option groups can be bound or unbound.
Page Break Control		Creates page breaks on forms. A page break forces the form to continue onto the next page when previewed or printed. This is an unbound control.

Components of the Control Group

Name	Button	Description
Combo Box Control		Inserts a control that combines the features of a text box and a list box. May be bound to the form's record source but may also use another record source to supply the list values. There is a **Combo Box Wizard** for this control.
Chart		Uses a **Chart Wizard** to create a bound or unbound chart. An unbound chart statically displays data while a bound chart updates as you step through records on the form.
Line Control		Inserts a line onto a form. Lines are useful for dividing a form into sections or for providing organization. This control is always unbound.
List Box Control		Adds a list box to the form. List boxes are similar to combo boxes except they do not have a text box area to support data entry. They may be bound to the form's record source but may also use another record source to supply the list values. This control can utilize the **List Box Wizard**.
Toggle Button Control		Creates a button that exists in one of two states: pressed in or pushed out. If bound, may only be bound to a field of the Yes/No data type. If created inside of a frame control, only one toggle button may be pressed in at a time.
Rectangle Control		Inserts a rectangle onto a form. Like lines, rectangles are useful for indicating that groups of controls belong together. This control is always unbound.
Check Box Control		Creates a check box that is similar to an option button. May exist in one of two (optionally three) states: checked or not checked (or *Null)*. If bound, may only be bound to a field of the Yes/No data type. If created inside of a frame control, only one check box may be checked at a time.
Unbound Object Frame		Inserts an unbound object frame. These frames display complex objects such as media clips or worksheets that are not associated with the form's record source. Always unbound.
Attachment		Manages *attachments* for any field of the *attachment* data type. Unbound attachment controls are disabled.

Components of the Control Group

Name	Button	Description
Option Button Control		Used to create an Option button. These are similar to a toggle button and may exist in one of two (optionally, three) states: selected or not selected (or *Null*). If bound, may only be bound to a field of the Yes/No data type. If created inside of a Frame control, only one option button may be selected at a time.
Subform/ Sub Report Control		Inserts a subform onto a form. The **Form Wizard** adds this control automatically when working with forms and multiple tables. The subform control is used mainly when you are creating forms and subforms manually. This control is always bound.
Bound Object Frame		Inserts a *bound* object frame. Unlike unbound object frames, this control displays complex objects such as images or media clips that are stored in the form's record source.
Image Control		Creates an image control that is used to display graphics files.
Set Control Defaults		Establishes a copy of the formatting that has been applied to the currently-selected control. This is a useful way to enforce a common design theme across all controls on a form, although once selected, it only applies to controls added *after* **Set Control Defaults** was activated.
Control Wizard		Starts a **Control Wizard** when activated and any of the following controls are selected and added to a form: Button, Option Group, Combo Box, Chart, List Box, or Subform.
ActiveX Controls		Inserts an *ActiveX* control onto the form. An *ActiveX* control is a subcomponent of another application, such as Internet Explorer or Windows Media Player. These objects are complex and have additional properties beyond those of the standard controls listed above. These may be bound to data but generally require some programming to elicit a record-by-record binding.

How to Add a Control from the Control Toolbox

The **Control** group includes the **Control Wizard**. When enabled, the wizard will start when you add certain control types to the form (see above). If you do not wish to work with the Wizard when it starts, simply choose **Cancel**. In most cases the control will be placed on the form as an *unbound* object. Other controls, such as the **Hyperlink**, **Web Browser**, and **Image** control will display helper dialogs regardless of the **Control Wizard** setting.

Step 1.   If the **Control** group is not displayed, choose the **Design** tab. Recall that only a subset of controls are displayed when in **Form Layout** view.

Step 2.   If desired, enable or disable the **Control Wizard** by selecting it. When the background color is light the control is enabled.

Step 3.   Select the desired control type. Refer to the table on page 59 for discussion of control types.

Step 4.   Position the mouse pointer over the approximate target location on the form.

Step 5.   Hold down the left mouse button and drag to create a rectangle that reflects the approximate final size of the control.

Step 6.   Release the left mouse button.

Step 7.   If a **Control Wizard** or a **Helper Dialog** box start, proceed according to the dialog box instructions. For most **Control Wizards** you can **Cancel** the operation which results in the creation of an unbound control.

Some controls that display text, such as **labels** and **Command buttons**, will immediately enter an **Edit Mode** where you can begin typing display text.

If you cancel a **Control Wizard** or a **Helper Dialog** and the control disappears, it isn't possible to manually configure the control. This applies to the **Chart** and **Unbound Object** controls.

Drawing controls is easiest when you apply a consistent drawing style. Most developers start in the upper left corner of the target region and draw the control to the right and downward.

Common Control Properties

Controls have fewer properties than forms, and the number of properties associated with a control varies between control types. For example, the **Label** control has no **Data** properties at all, reflecting the fact that labels cannot be bound.

Despite these facts, there is a group of control properties that developers tend to use frequently. The following table identifies these properties. Properties having significant implications for individual control types will be addressed when discussing individual control types in Chapter 6, beginning on page 83.

 When you modify a control's formatting attributes by using the **Format** tab, the **Property Sheet** is automatically updated.

Common Control Format Properties

Property	Description
Caption	Sets the display text for controls such as labels and command buttons.
Visible	Controls whether a control is visible.
Width	Specifies the control's width.
Height	Specifies the control's height.
Top	Indicates the position of the top of the control relative to the upper left corner of the form. Units are the same as for the **Left** property.
Left	Indicates the position of the left side of the control relative to the upper left corner of the form. You can express the values in any common unit of measurement such as 0.2 in or 34 cm.
Back Style	Controls whether the background in the control is transparent or not (normal). Normal is the default.
Back Color	Sets the color of the control background. Only available if the **Back Style** property is set to *Normal*.
Border Style	Controls the style of the border line around a control.
Border Width	Sets the width of the border line.
Border Color	Sets the color of the border line.
Special Effect	Specifies whether the control has any special effects such as raised, sunken, or etched. The default value varies between control types.
Font Name	Sets the font for controls that display text.
Font Size	Specifies the font size for controls that display text.
Font Weight	Sets the font weight (thickness of the characters) for controls that display text. The **Bold** value is analogous to applying the **Bond** font attribute to the text.
Font Italic	Sets **Italic** on or off for controls which display text.
Font Underline	Sets **Underline** on or off for controls which display text.
Fore Color	Controls the font color for controls that display text.

Common Control Data Properties

Property	Description
Control Source	Indicates the field that the control is bound to. If blank, the control is unbound.
Text Format	Specifies the format the control uses to display data. This property can be inherited from the bound field.
Default Value	Sets the default value displayed by the control. This property can be inherited from the bound field.
Validation Rule	Specifies the rule the control uses to validate data entry. This property can be inherited from the bound field.
Validation Text	Sets the text message displayed if the validation rule is violated. This property can be inherited from the bound field.
Enabled	Controls whether the control can receive *focus*. When set to *False* the control appears dimmed and will not respond to mouse or keyboard actions.
Locked	Controls whether the control can respond to mouse or keyboard actions. When set to *True*, the control appears normal but will not accept edits or new data.

Some **Data** properties may be inherited from a bound control's field. These properties may be made to be different from the field's settings, although for properties such as **Validation Rule** and **Input Mask** you may render data entry impossible with multiple properties established. This is true because tables always enforce their field properties even if data entry is via a form.

Common Control Other Properties

Property	Description
Name	Sets the name of the control. This is different from the **Caption** property of controls. Most developers name controls in a manner that reflects their function.
ControlTip Text	Sets the text that appears in a *Screen Tip* when the mouse is held still for at least 1 second over the control.
Tab Index	Specifies the ordinal position of the control in the form's *tab sequence*. Example: if the **Tab Index** for a control is *3*, it will be the third control to gain focus when the user starts at the top of the form and repeatedly uses the *Tab* key.
Tab Stop	Indicates whether the control can receive the *focus* as a result of using the *Tab* key.
Status Bar Text	Specifies the text that appears on the **Status Bar** when the control receives the *focus*. For bound controls, this is inherited from the field's **Description** property.
Shortcut Menu Bar	Names the custom shortcut menu that appears if the user right-clicks on the control.
Help Context ID	For forms that utilize custom help, this property is used to open the correct help topic for the control.

Selecting Controls

Controls are most easily added, moved, sized, and modified by using the mouse. The majority of manipulations involve using the mouse pointer to select a specific region of the control, depending upon the desired action.

Many controls, such as text boxes, option buttons, and check boxes have attached labels. These are separate label controls but under most circumstances they behave as if they were linked to the parent control. Selecting an attached label separate from its parent control requires a slightly different procedure.

How to Select a Control

Step 1.   Position the mouse pointer over the control and click once, or from the **Format** tab, **Selection** group, choose the desired object from the control drop down box.

To select a label that is attached to some other control, position the mouse pointer over the label, not the parent control

About Selected Controls and the Mouse Pointer

There are several actions you can take against a selected control, including moving, deleting, or resizing the control. If working with an attached control (a label and its parent control), you can act upon the controls together or individually, depending upon which control you actually select.

When a control or a set of attached controls is selected, the mouse pointer will change shape over various regions to indicate the actions possible. The following illustrations highlight the various *handles* and the mouse pointer shapes you will encounter.

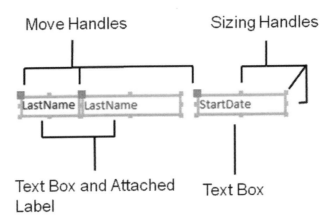

Object	Description
Move Handles	Moves controls individually. Manipulating the **Move Handle** will not move an attached control and its parent together, nor will it move a group of selected controls. **Move Handles** are always used to move controls individually.
Sizing Handles	Resizes controls. If an attached label and its parent control are selected, manipulating a **Sizing Handle** will size both controls. If working with a group of selected controls, manipulating a **Sizing Handle** will resize every selected control. The top center and bottom center **Sizing Handles** are used to adjust the control height. Working with the left center or right center **Sizing Handles** will adjust control width. Selecting any of the corner **Sizing Handles** will proportionately adjust the control's height and width.

Mouse Pointer Shapes in Design View

Shape	Description
	Select pointer - used to select objects.
	Text insertion pointer - enters text-edit mode when clicked.
	Move pointer. Moves a single control when over a **Move Handle**. Moves two or more controls (when selected) over any control.
	Resize right/left (width) or **top/bottom** (height), respectively.
	Resize Diagonal (both height and width), depending upon the corner selected and the drag direction.

How to Use Edit Mode

This mode can be used to change the text displayed in **Labels** and on **Command Buttons**. You can also use **Edit Mode** to change or edit the **Control Source** property of **Text**, **List**, and **Combo Boxes**.

Step 1.   Select the desired control.

Step 2.   With the control selected, position the mouse pointer over the control's text area.

Step 3.   When the mouse pointer appears as a **Text Insertion** pointer, click once on the control.

Step 4.   Make edits to the control's text as desired.

Step 5.   Leave **Edit Mode** by selecting some other object on the form, or press the *Enter* key.

 If you wish to create multiple lines of text while in **Edit Mode**, use the *Ctrl + Enter* key combination to insert a new line. Note that you may need to adjust the control size to view all of the text.

How to Select Groups of Controls

This method works best when you need to select controls that cleanly fall within the rectangular selection area.

Step 1. Position the mouse pointer near one of the target controls. Ensure that the mouse pointer shape is the **Select** shape.

Step 2. Hold down the left mouse button and drag a rectangle that encloses or touches all the desired controls.

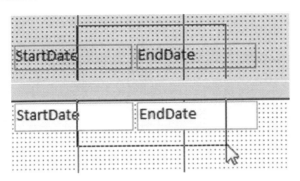

Step 3. Release the mouse button. Depending upon settings described in the note box below, the controls entirely within or touched by the rectangle will be selected.

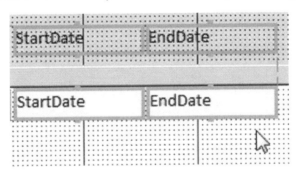

 The behavior of the drawn rectangle to select controls it touches versus selecting only those controls fully contained within the rectangle is specified by the **Access Options** dialog box. From the **File** tab, choose **Options**, then choose **Object Designers**. In the **Form/Report Design View** area, adjust the **Selection behavior** settings.

How to Select Groups of Non-Adjacent Controls

Step 1. Use the mouse pointer to select the first desired control.

Step 2. Hold down the *Shift* key while selecting additional controls.

Step 3. Release the *Shift* when done.

How to Select Groups of Controls Using the Ruler

Use this method when the desired controls are all arranged vertically or horizontally.

Step 1.   To select a horizontal stack of controls, position the mouse over the **Horizontal Ruler**

or, to select a vertical line of controls, position the mouse over the **Vertical Ruler**.

Step 2.   When the mouse pointer changes to a dark arrow, hold down the left mouse button.

Step 3.   If selecting a horizontal stack of controls, drag the **Selection Rectangle** right or left to include the desired controls, or if selecting a vertical line of controls, drag the **Selection Rectangle** up or down to include the desired controls.

Step 4.   Release the mouse button.

 A single click on the horizontal ruler will select all controls directly below that point. A single click on the vertical ruler will select all controls directly to the left of that point. This selection method selects controls across all form sections.

Moving, Sizing, and Aligning Controls

You can modify the position, size, and alignment of controls either individually or as a group of selected controls. Some actions, such as aligning or resizing controls relative to an existing control, are available only as menu commands. When moving or resizing controls you should pay mind to the shape of the mouse pointer (discussed on page 67) as it informs you about the particular mode the mouse is in.

How to Move Controls

Step 1.   To move an individual control, position the mouse pointer over the **Move Handle** so it changes to the **Move** pointer, or to move an attached label and its parent control, or to move a group of selected controls, position the mouse pointer over the control (anywhere except the **Move** Handle) so it changes to the **Move** pointer.

Step 2.   Hold down the left mouse button and drag the control or controls to a new location.

Step 3.   Release the mouse button.

How to Delete an Attached Label

Controls such as **Text Boxes** always appear with an attached **Label**. There are situations where you may wish to retain the data bound control yet delete the associated **Label**.

Step 1.   If the control is already selected, click on the **Detail** section to unselect it.

Step 2.   Click on the **Label** (not the attached bound control). The distinction between the entire label and bound control being selected verses only the label being selected is illustrated below.

Both label and bound control selected:

Only label selected:

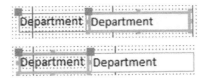

Step 3.   Once the desired label is selected, press *Delete*.

It is possible to delete the label associated with a bound control but not to delete the bound control and retain the label.

How to Move a Control and/or its Attached Label to a Different Form Section

If you are creating a form from scratch, or modifying an existing form, you may come across situations where you wish to place a label associated with a bound control in a different section (a common example is to move the control label to the **Form Header** area. You may also find the need to move a control from one form section to another (for example from the **Form Footer** to the **Form Header** section). Access does not permit the simple dragging of a control or its attached label to a different section. If you attempt such a move you'll notice that the control cannot cross a section boundary. You must cut and paste either the entire control pair or the label to effect this type of move.

Step 1.   If your intent is to move a control/label pair, select the entire control. If, instead you wish to only move an attached label, select only the label part of the control. Use the illustrations from the previous procedure as a guide.

Step 2.   Cut the selected control by pressing *Ctrl + x*.

Step 3.   Select the target section. For example if you are moving a control to the **Form Header** section, click once on the **Form Header** bar located above that section.

Step 4.   Paste the selected control by pressing *Ctrl + v*.

Step 5.   The pasted control will appear in the upper left corner of the target section (it may appear floating over other controls in that area). Drag the selected control to the desired location within the target section.

To undo this type of move, press *Ctrl + z*.

How to Resize Controls Using the Mouse

Step 1.   Select the control or controls you wish to resize.

Step 2.   To resize the width of the control or controls, position the mouse pointer over a left or right center **Sizing Handle**, or to resize the height of the control or controls, position the mouse pointer over a top or bottom center **Sizing Handle,** or to proportionately resize the control or controls, position the mouse pointer over a corner **Sizing Handle**.

Step 3.   Hold down the left mouse button and drag the mouse in the direction that reflects the desired size of the control or controls.

Step 4.   Release the mouse button.

Double-clicking on a **Sizing Handle** for **Label** or **Text Controls** will automatically resize the control to fit the text it displays. Double-clicking elsewhere on the control opens the **Property Sheet**.

For fine adjustments you may want to key numeric values into the **Height** or **Width** property of the control. These properties are located on the **Format** tab of the **Property Sheet**. Similarly, the **Top** and **Left** properties control placement on the form relative to the top left corner of the section the control is in.

How to Resize a Group of Selected Controls Relative to one of the Controls

This method only applies when two or more controls are selected.

Step 1.   Select the controls you wish to resize.

Step 2.   From the **Arrange** tab, in the **Sizing &** Ordering group, choose **Size/Space**.

Step 3.   Choose the desired size option.

Option	Description
To Fit	Proportionately resizes the controls so each best fits its contents.
To Tallest	Resizes all controls so their height is equal to the tallest control in the selected group.
To Shortest	Resizes all controls so their height is equal to the shortest control in the selected group.
To Grid	Resizes controls so their corners each touch a grid intersection. The grid size is set through the **Grid X** and **Grid Y** properties of the form.
To Widest	Resizes all controls so their width is equal to the widest control in the selected group.
To Narrowest	Resizes all controls so their width is equal to the narrowest control in the selected group.

How to Align a Group of Selected Controls

This method only applies when two or more controls are selected.

Step 1.   Select the controls you wish to resize.

Step 2.   From the **Arrange** tab, in the **Sizing &** Ordering group, choose **Align**.

Step 3.   Choose the desired align option.

Option	Description
To Grid	Aligns the top left corner of each selected control to the nearest point on the grid.
Left	Aligns the left side of each selected control with the left side of the left-most control.
Right	Aligns the right side of each selected control with the right side of the right-most control.
Top	Aligns the top of each selected control with the top side of the top-most control.
Bottom	Aligns the bottom of each selected control with the bottom of the bottom-most control.

How to Automatically Adjust Control Spacing

If the selection includes three or more controls, spacing is equalized first before adjustments are made to the controls.

Step 1.   Select the controls you wish to resize.

Step 2.   From the **Arrange** tab, in the **Sizing &** Ordering group, choose **Size/Space**.

Step 3.   Choose the desired spacing option.

Horizontal and Vertical Spacing Options

Option	Description
Equal Horizontal	Equalizes the horizontal spacing between three or more controls. If only two controls are selected this option has no effect.
Increase Horizontal	Increases horizontal spacing between controls by one grid point.
Decrease Horizontal	Decreases horizontal spacing between controls by one grid point.
Equal Vertical	Equalizes the vertical spacing between three or more controls. If only two controls are selected this option has no effect.
Increase Vertical	Increases vertical spacing between controls by one grid point.
Decrease Vertical	Decreases vertical spacing between controls by one grid point.

How to Group Controls

You can group two or more controls so they always behave as a consolidated unit. Once controls have been grouped, you can ungroup them to restore their individual aspects.

Step 1.   Select two or more controls.

Step 2.   From the **Sizing & Ordering** group on the **Arrange** tab, choose **Size/Space**, then select **Group**.

 Once controls have been grouped, selecting a single member of the group selects all members. To ungroup controls, first select the group, repeat the procedure above except choose **Ungroup** from the **Size/Space** drop down box.

Formatting Controls

The format properties of a control are probably the most commonly used control attributes. Access provides two methods for adjusting format properties - you can use the **Property Sheet** or make adjustments via the **Format** tab while in either **Form Layout** or **Form Design View**. The latter contains groups that focus on the most common control format attributives such as font and border styles.

All format attributes for the currently-selected control on a form (or a report) are available from the **Format** tab on the **Property Sheet**. As we will see in Chapter 6, format properties will vary between control types but for many controls there remains a common set of formatting attributes and these generally map to the options available on the **Format** tab. The following table outlines the controls on this tab.

Format Tab

Group	Description
Selection	Select a single control using the drop down box or use **Select All** for applying an attribute broadly.
Font	Offers the most common font properties such as font name, font size, and attributes such as bold or italic. This group also offers a **Format Painter** which works similarly to the painter in other Office Suite members.
Number	Common attributes for number, currency, and date/time data types.
Background	Set a background image for the current form or report, or if the **Detail** section (or a group when working with reports) is selected, set **Alternate Row Color**.
Control Formatting	Set **Quick Styles** or **Change Shape** for **Command** and **Toggle Buttons**, apply **Conditional Formatting** (discussed later in this Chapter) or adjust properties of lines, borders, and background for some control types.

Not all format attributes are available for the currently-selected control. This is true both for the **Format** tab, where options may appear disabled, and the **Property Sheet** where a format attribute may not be listed.

The **Format** tab and the **Property Sheet** are always synchronized. If you select a control and then apply a format attribute using either the **Format** tab or the **Property Sheet**, the complimentary control will also update to reflect the format change.

Control Defaults

Depending upon which version of Microsoft Access you are using, when you place a control such as a **Text Box** on a form or report, it is created with certain default format properties. For example, **Text Boxes** in Microsoft Access 2010 appear with the default font *Calibri 11point* and a font color of *Black, Text 1,Lighter 25%*. This behavior is applicable to reports as well. If you choose not to use a specific theme (or chose not to create a custom theme) you can override these control defaults on a form-by-form or report-by-report basis.

Access also permits you to choose a form or report in a specific database which will serve as the default prototype for *all* Access databases. Unfortunately there isn't a middle ground approach where a specific form or report serves as the template for all other forms or reports but only within the context of the current database. So when you assign a new set of default format properties on a form or report, you must repeat this procedure for any new forms or reports in your database if you wish to apply a particular look and feel.

How to Assign a Control Default

Use this procedure after you have modified the format properties on any control on the current form or report. These settings will apply to all new controls of that particular control type, but only as they relate to the current form or report. Control defaults only apply to visual attributes such as font, border styles, and fore and background colors.

Step 1.   Working in **Form Design View**, add the desired control type to your form.

Step 2.   Adjust the format properties (mainly using the **Font** and **Control Formatting** options on the **Format** tab.

Step 3.   On the **Design** tab, in the **Controls** group, click on the **More** arrow and select **Set Control Defaults**.

Step 4.   Any new control you add of the same control type will inherit the design changes you made in Step 2.

There is no easy way to unset a control default back to the original form. You must manually modify format properties to duplicate those that apply to the same control type on a new form or report and then repeat Step 3 above.

Conditional Formatting of Controls

The **Text Box** and **Combo Box** controls both support conditional formatting, both for forms and reports. With this feature you can set conditions which, if met, change format attributes for the control or format a **Data Bar** that graphically relates the value in the current control to some minimum and maximum values (generally as they relate to all records in the bound field). Conditional formatting is a great way to create controls that alert the end user when a value is out of bounds, unusually low or high, or otherwise requires attention. For example, you can create a control that changes font color to red whenever a project budget value exceeds some minimum value.

How to Apply Conditional Formatting

You must be in either **Form Layout** or **Form Design View** to apply conditional formatting.

Step 1   Select the desired **Text Box** or **Combo Box** control.

Step 2.   From the **Format** tab, in the **Control Formatting** group, select **Conditional Formatting**. The **Conditional Formatting Rules Manager** will appear as follows:

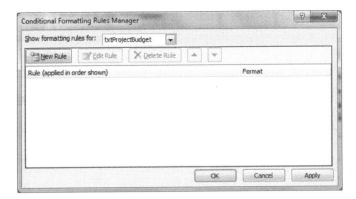

Step 3.   Choose **New Rule**. The **New Formatting Rule** dialog box will appear:

Step 4.   Accept the default rule type (check values in the current record or use an expression). Move to the **Edit the rule description** area.

Step 5.   Adjust the settings using the following table as a guide. Note that the value of the second combo box will dictate how many range boxes appear.

Left to Right Control Order	Description
First combo box	Determines whether to base the conditional rule on field value, the value of an expression, or simply whether the control has focus.
Second combo box	Sets the range of the condition. Choose from options such as *Between, Greater than, equals,* etc.
Range boxes (1 or 2 present)	If working with field values, use the first and/or second range box to specify the numeric range. If creating a rule such as *Greater than*, use the single range box to set a specific number or expression. If working with an expression in the first combo box, use this box to create the comparative expression.
Format controls	Use these to set which format attributes change if the rule condition is met. You can set font attributes such as bold or font color, background color, or enable/disable the control.

Step 6.   Adjust the rule and format controls as desired. Choose **OK** when finished. In the following illustration, the value of a text box named *txtProjectBudget* has been set to turn the font color *Red* if the displayed budget is *Greater than* $25,000.

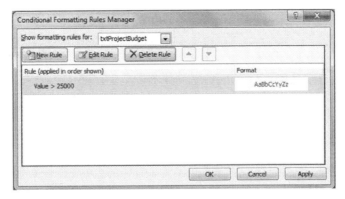

Step 7.   If you desire additional rules for the current control, select **New Rule** and repeat Steps 4 through 6. An example of a second rule, which changes the *Background* color to *Red* if the project budget is over $50,000 is illustrated below.

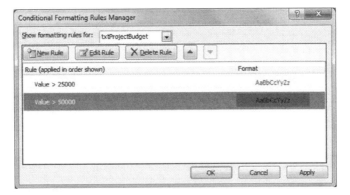

Warning: Access processes multiple rules for a single control in the order displayed in the **Conditional Formatting Rules Manager**. Note that in the preceding illustration projects with budgets in excess of $50,000 will *never* format as expected since the first rule's condition would be met first. In cases such as these, change the rule order by selecting a rule and using the **Move Up** or **Move Down** arrows to rearrange their order.

How to Apply a Data Bar

Data Bars work best when used on forms that have a simple and direct relationship to an underlying table. If you attempt to create a data bar on a form or report that pulls data from several tables, Access will inform you that data bars may only be applied to tables and queries. This misleading error really reflects the case that this formatting type is best suited for single table relationships.

Step 1. Begin by repeating Steps 1-3 from the previous procedure. When the **New Formatting Rule** dialog box appears, choose **Compare to other records**. The dialog box will change appearance and should look like the following image:

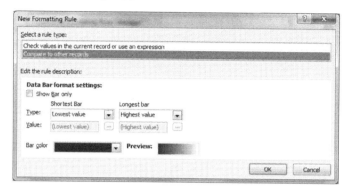

Step 2. Use the following table as a guide to create your data bar. When finished, choose **OK**.

Option	Description
Show Bar only	If checked, only the data bar (and not the field value) will display.
Type	Choose from *Lowest value*, *Value*, or *Percent*. These settings represent the smallest and largest values for your data bar. For example, in order to relate some field value against all records, you would accept the default *Lowest Value* and *Highest Value* settings. To create a threshold or to rank against percentages, choose those options instead.
Value	Disabled if you choose *Lowest* and *Highest Value*, otherwise enter a low and high value to act as the thresholds for your data bar.
Bar color	Select the color for the data bar. You may also need to adjust the **Font Color** to improve visibility.

Step 3. Close the editor by selecting **OK**. An example of a simple form that compares individual project budgets between two people is illustrated below. In this case the data bar is displaying the current budget against the smallest and largest individual budgets in the underlying table data.

Staff   Jones

Project Server upgrade

Budget $500.00

Staff	Kidwell
Project	Server upgrade
Budget	$40,000.00

How to Edit a Conditional Format

Both conditional formats and data bars may be modified once created.

Step 1.   Open the form or report in **Layout** or **Design** view and select the desired control.

Step 2.   From the **Format** tab, in the **Control Formatting** group, select **Conditional Formatting**.

Step 3.   Select the desired rule (if more than one are present for the current control), then choose **Edit Rule**.

Step 4.   Proceed working with the **New Formatting Rule** dialog box as outlined in the two previous procedures.

Changing Control Type

It is possible to change many controls from one type to another. The list of available choices to choose from depends upon the original control type. For example, a **Label control** may only be converted into a **Text Box**, while an **Option Button** may be changed into either a **Check Box** or a **Toggle Button** control.

When a control is converted from one type to another, Access will copy those properties shared by both controls. If the original control type has properties not found in the target control type, those properties are lost. If the target control type has properties not found in the original control, the default settings for those properties are used.

How to Change a Control Type

Step 1.   Select the desired control.

Step 2.   Right-click and from the **Shortcut** menu, choose **Change To**.

Step 3.   Choose the desired target control type. The following table outlines the options. If the control type isn't listed it isn't possible to change its type.

Control Type	Change To
Label	Text Box.
Text Box	Label, List Box, Combo Box.
Hyperlink	Text Box, Image, Command Button.
Combo Box	Text Box, List Box
Toggle Button	Check Box, Option Button
Check Box	Toggle button, Option Button
Unbound Object Frame	Image
Radio Button	Toggle Button, Check Box

Controlling Tab Order

When a form is in either **Form** view or **Form Layout** view, a control has the *focus* when the operating system acts upon it when the user presses a key or selects the control using the mouse. Typically, controls containing text display an *insertion cursor* when they have focus. **Command, Option,** and **Toggle Buttons** display a highlighted halo and **Combo** and **List Boxes** display selected text.

Any control you place on a form which can gain *focus* has a **Tab Stop** and **Tab Index** property.

- The Tab Stop property controls whether a control can gain focus when the user presses the Tab or Enter key, or uses an Arrow key to move the focus between controls.

- If the Tab Stop property is set to Yes (the default), then the Tab Index property sets the focus order of controls on the form. Access ensures that no two controls on a single form may have the same Tab Index property.

The *Tab Order* is generally the order in which each control was placed on the form. During development of a form it is possible to end up with a tab order that doesn't flow naturally and can cause some confusion among end users of your form. Thus, it is good design to ensure that the tab order on a form is logical and moves the user between controls in a logical sequence. Generally this means ensuring that the direction of the tab order progresses either down and then across, or over and then down.

Although you can manipulate the **Tab Index** property manually for each control, many developers use the **Tab Order** dialog box for this purpose.

How to Control Tab Order

The form must be open in **Form Design** view.

Step 1.   From the **Tools** group on the **Design** tab, **Tab Order**. A dialog box similar to the following will appear:

Option	Description
Section	Specifies which form section's controls will be listed in the **Custom Order** list.
Custom Order	Lists the controls in the form section specified in the **Section** area. You can drag one or more controls to a new order in the list to change the tab order.
Auto Order	Automatically arranges a tab order using a left-to-right, top-to-bottom scheme. Only the controls in the section indicated in the **Section** area are affected.

Step 2.   Select the appropriate form section in the **Section** area.

Step 3.   Select a control to reorder from the **Custom Order** list and drag it to a new position in the list.

Step 4.   Continue Step 3 until the desired controls have been reordered.

Step 5.   Choose **OK.**

Chapter 6 | A Tour of Form Controls

The previous chapter introduced to you the generalities concerning controls, including their common properties, selection and sizing/moving techniques. In this chapter we will focus specifically on control types and discuss how to work with controls. Controls will be introduced in the order of their relative usefulness. This is certainly a subjective approach but this order is derived from years of the author's development using Microsoft Access. We will tour the most commonly used bound controls, followed by a series of controls that organize or order parts of a form. Additional, bound controls that serve highly specialized tasks will then be covered.

Where a control is associated with a **Control Wizard** we'll introduce the Wizard approach first followed by instructions for manually working with a control and its properties. Whereas some of the Wizards in Microsoft Access are of dubious worth (the **Simple Query Wizard** comes to mind), the Wizards associated with controls are very helpful.

Text Box Control

The **Text Box** control is used to display text. It can display a single line or multiple lines and is therefore a good candidate for displaying field values from a *Memo* field. For most databases, the most common data type is text. Every text, memo, date/time, number, currency, hyperlink and calculated data type resolves by default to a text box on a form.

Text Boxes are generally used for two purposes on a form:

- As a bound control, they display field data in an underlying field from the form's record source.

- As calculated controls, they may display expressions. In this mode, the Control Source property (or the displayed text within the Text Box) must begin with an equals sign (=). Calculated controls are discussed in Chapter 7.

When you add a **Text Box** to a form, it includes an attached **Label**. If the **Text Box** is bound, the label displays the bound field name, otherwise it displays a value such as *Text8*, (the name of the new **Text Box**)which Access applies to ensure uniqueness among controls. This **Label** may be removed from the **Text Box**, if desired, by selecting it separately from the **Text Box** and pressing the *Delete* key.

Important Text Box Control Properties

Property	Description
Control Source	Names the field if the control is bound, or contains an *expression* if the field is unbound. Expressions must always begin with an **equals sign** (=).
Input Mask	Specifies the manner in which data may be entered into the text box.
Format	Controls how the data are displayed in the text box. This property is useful for formatting numeric data.
Show Date Picker	By default, set to *Yes* if the **Text Box** is bound to a date/time field. When set to *Yes* a date picker appears whenever the **Text Box** gains the focus.
Scroll Bars	Specifies whether the **Text Box** displays a vertical scroll bar. The default is *None*.
Can Grow	Controls whether the **Text Box** can increase in size vertically to fully display its contents when the form is printed. This property has no effect in other form views. This property is frequently used in Reports.
Can Shrink	Controls whether the **Text Box** can decrease in size vertically to best fit its contents when the form is printed. This property has no effect in other form views. This property is frequently used in Reports.
Allow AutoCorrect	Specifies whether *AutoCorrect* is enabled when entering data into the **Text Box**. The default is *Yes*.

To edit the contents of a **Text Box** you should be in **Form Design View**. Single click in the text area itself - the mouse pointer should change to a **Text Insertion Pointer** (see page 67). Click a second time to enter edit mode. It is *not* recommended that you edit the contents of a *bound* control as the effect will be to disconnect the **Text Box** from its **Control Source**.

Points on Working with Text Boxes

- It is best practice to apply **Format Masks**, **Default Values**, and **Validation Rules** at the level of the table. When defined as part of a table, any bound text box inherits those settings. If you define these properties at the level of the **Text Box** and they differ from those settings applied at the table level, the **Text Box** can cause a conflict with the table.

- To create a **Text Box** that displays data but isn't editable, set its **Enabled** property (**Data** tab) to *No*. This will gray out the **Text Box** and prevent the focus from entering the control.

- If you create a single-line **Text Box**, ensure that the **Scroll Bars** property is set to *None*. Use **Scroll Bars** only for **Text Boxes** that have been adjusted to display multiple lines of text. This is especially important if the **Text Box** is bound to a **Memo** field.

- If you want a **Text Box** to appear *without* its **Label**, select the **Label** separately and press *Delete.*

- If you make format changes to a **Text Box** and wish to apply these changes to all *additional* **Text Boxes** added to the form, select the **Text Box**, then from the **Controls** group on the **Design** tab, select **Set Control Defaults**.

- Many format properties can be applied to a **Text Box** by using the **Format** tab. Changes applied to the **Text Box** automatically update in the appropriate *Property* setting.

- **Text Boxes** may become *calculated* controls by entering an *expression* either directly into the control or by specifying an expression in the **Control Source** property. Calculated controls are discussed in Chapter 7.

Label Control

Aa **Label** controls are the same regardless of whether drawn manually using the **Label** control tool or attached to an **Option Group, Text Box, Combo Box, List Box,** or **Subform** control. In all cases where a **Label** appears attached to another control, you may select the **Label** separately to move it or delete it from the form.

A label that is associated with another control (such as a **Text Box** or a **Subform**) can serve as the *Accelerator Key* for that object (even though **Labels**, by definition, cannot receive the focus). By including an *Ampersand* (&) before the desired letter in the **Label** caption the letter will appear in **Form** or **Form Layout View** with an underbar (_). This is a visual cue that using the *Alt +* *accelerator letter* combination will move to focus to the label's parent control. For example, if the **Caption** property for a label is specified as: *First &Name* the label will appear as the following in **Form** view:

First Name   Amanda

Pressing *Alt N* would place the focus in the associated **Text Box**.

Important Label Control Properties

Property	Description
Caption	Specifies the text that is displayed by the **Label** control.
Name	Sets the name of the control.
Display When	Indicates whether the control is always displayed, or only displayed when the form is viewed (Screen Only) or printed (Print Only). The default is *Always*.

Points on Working with Labels

- With the exception of the use of *Accelerator keys*, **Labels** cannot receive focus and therefore do not have a **Tab Stop** property.

- A **Label** may never be bound or include an expression. Entering something like *=Date()* (which in the **Control Source** property of a **Text Box** would result in the display of the current date) in the **Caption** property of a **Label** would result in the display of the literal expression *=Date()*.

- If you make format changes to a **Label** and wish to apply these changes to all *additional* labels added to the form, select the **Label**, then from the **Controls** group on the **Design** tab, select **Set Control Defaults**.

- Many format properties can be applied to a **Label** by using the **Format** tab. Changes applied to the **Label** automatically update in the appropriate *Property* setting.

- Double-clicking on a **Label** control enters **Edit Mode**. In this mode you can enter, edit, or delete the text displayed in the **Label**. Note that this action modifies the **Label** control's **Caption** property.

- Double-clicking on a **Sizing Handle** automatically adjusts the **Height** and **Width** properties such that the label is sized only to display the current **Caption**.

- To create multiple-line **Labels**, start a new line by pressing ***Shift + Enter*** when entering text directly in the **Label** or when specifying the **Caption** property.

Combo Box and List Box Controls

A **Combo Box** control combines a **Text Box** and a **List Box** in a single control (hence its name). You can either enter text into the text box portion of the control, or use the drop-down list and select a value. An example of a combo box which has been opened to display list values appears below.

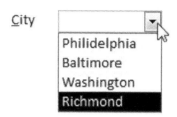

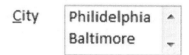

A **List Box** is similar to a **Combo Box** but does not permit data entry into the control. You use a **List Box** when you need to enforce selection of data from another data source or from a custom list. An example of a **List Box**, using the same record source as above, would appear similar to the following on a form opened in **Form View**:

Combo Box and **List Box** controls can display lists which are derived from an existing table or query, or are custom created. When a user chooses from the list, the selected value can be stored in the control's *bound* field or stored as a value of the **Combo** or **List Box** (in the latter case the control is unbound). If a **Combo** or **List Box** is unbound the developer must use VBA programming (using the control's **Value** property) to incorporate the selected value into a meaningful context. If you do not intend to incorporate VBA programming code you are best off creating *bound* **Combo** or **List Box** controls.

Both controls are excellent devices for limiting data entry. When a user is either given a list to choose from (with the option of creating a new entry), or is forced to choose from a list, the likelihood of a data entry error is reduced, or in the case of forcing a choice from a list, eliminated altogether.

An important point about these two control types, especially when compared to a **Text Box** control, is the interplay between where these controls get their display data versus how they store bound data. With a **Text Box**, the only bound property you work with is the **Control Source**. This property mediates both the display of the bound data and any deletions or edits you make to that data. This is different than a **Combo** or **List Box** where additional properties, **Row Source** and **Row Source Type** specify *where* the displayed data are coming from. These properties are unique to these two control types. The important properties of these controls, as they relate to the display and management of data, are outlined in the following tables.

Important Combo and List Box Data Properties

Property	Description
Control Source	Sets the bound field for the control or, if the control unbound displays a blank value. If unbound, any selected item in the **Combo** or **List Box** is stored in a property named *value* and is available as long as the form remains open. If the control is bound when a change is made to the displayed data the field specified by the **Control Source** is updated.
Row Source	Unique to **Combo** and **List Boxes**, this property specifies where the control gets its display data. The data may come from an existing table or query, or may be a manually-entered *value list*. If bound to a table or query, the property typically contains a **SQL** statement. If set to a value list, the list items, delimited by double quotes and separated by semicolons, is displayed.
Row Source Type	Also unique to these two controls. Choices are *Table/Query* or *Value List*. Ensure that this setting agrees with the value(s) present in the **Row Source** property or Access will generate an error if you attempt to use the control. If you choose *Table/Query* then the **Row Source** must name a table, query, or a SQL statement. If using *Value List* then **Row Source** must be a semicolon-delimited list of values.
Limit to List	Permits new data entry directly in the **Combo Box**. Not a property of **List Boxes**. The default value is *Yes*.
Allow Value List Edits	Permits data entry for a **Combo** or **List Box** when the **Row Source Type** property is set to *Value List*. The default setting is *Yes*. Note that if you wish to restrict data entry you should set this property to *No*.
List Items Edit Form	Specifies the form to open if you've permitted users to add new list items via the **Allow Value List Edits**. If left blank, Access provides a default data entry form.
Inherit Value List	Enables inheritance of a value list when a **Combo** or **List Box** is bound to a field that itself is a lookup data type. The default value is *Yes*.
Allow Multiple Values	If set to *Yes*, permits selection of multiple data values (note that this violates first normal form in a database!). Values are stored in the field as comma-separated entries.
Show Only Row Source Values	If **Allow Multiple Values** is set to *Yes* this property behaves like **Limit to List**.

Combo and **List Boxes** can display one or more columns of data, and this is a useful way to ensure that your end users are getting the information necessary to make the correct selection. As an example, imagine a staff table that contains separate first, middle, and last name fields, as well as a StaffID primary key field. You can configure a **Combo** or **List Box** to display staff last name, first name, and middle name fields so users can be sure they are selecting the correct staff member. Regardless of how many columns are displayed, only one column can serve as the data source for the **Control Source** property (if the control is bound) or the **Value** property (if the control is unbound). The following table outlines the properties that control column formatting.

Important Combo and List Format Properties

Property	Description
Column Count	Sets the total number of columns the control will contain, as specified by the value in the **Row Source** property. This is not related to the number of columns visible - see the next property.
Column Widths	The width of the columns, for multiple-column controls, each width separated by semicolons. If a column is hidden, it's width is set to zero.
Column Heads	Specifies whether column headings are present. If so, the first values from the **Row Source** property appear as headings.
List Rows	For a **Combo Box**, sets the number of rows visible when the drop down box is activated.
List Width	For a **Combo Box**, sets the width of the display area visible when the drop down box is activated. This value can be different from the control's **Width** property and is useful when several columns must be displayed. For a **List Box**, the **Width** property controls how wide the control and display area are.
Bound Column	The number of the column that the control is bound to.

With some of these properties identified, we'll discuss how to use a **Combo Box** Wizard to create one of three control types. The process is identical for **List Boxes** so we'll only focus on creating **Combo Boxes**. Following discussion of Wizards, we will detail how to create these controls manually and provide examples of the important properties you should work with.

Using the Combo or List Box Wizard

The **Combo** or **List Box Wizard** gives you three choices when creating a **Combo** or **List Box**. You can:

- Create a bound control that displays list values from an existing table or query. When the user makes a choice from the list, that value is stored in the Combo Box's bound field or, if creating an unbound control, in a value field.

- Create a bound control that displays a custom list you create when working with the wizard. The list becomes a property of the Combo Box control and may be edited. When the user makes a choice from the list, that value is stored in the Combo Box's bound field or, if creating an unbound control, in a value field.

- Make a combo box that lists field values from the form's record source. When the user chooses a value, the form jumps to that record. This choice creates an unbound Combo or List Box.

We'll step through all three options using a **Combo Box** as the target control. The process of working with a **List Box** and this Wizard is the same.

How to Use the Combo Box Control Wizard to Create a Control That Uses Table or Query Values

This is a great approach when you wish to reduce the number of data entry errors. By forcing the user to select from a determined list the possibility of typographical errors during data entry is greatly reduced.

Step 1.   Enable the **Control Wizard**.

Step 2.   Select the **Combo Box** control.

Step 3.   Draw a **Combo Box** onto the form. The first dialog box of the **Combo Box Wizard** will appear similar to the following:

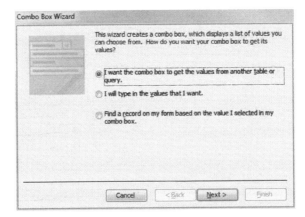

Step 4.   Choose the option **I want the combo box to look up the values in a table or query**. Choose **Next**. The second dialog box of the **Combo Box Wizard** will appear similar to the following:

Step 5. Adjust the **View** settings if desired, and then select the table or query that contains the appropriate values. Choose **Next**. The third dialog box of the **Combo Box Wizard** will appear similar to the following:

Step 6. Use the **Add (>)** or **Add all (>>)** button to add one or more fields to the **Selected Fields** list. Although several fields may be displayed on the **Combo Box** list, only one of the fields may be used to supply data to the bound field. (For the purposes of this example, both fields will be added). Choose **Next**.

Step 7. Select any fields you wish to sort (you can choose up to 4). This step only affects the display sort order on the **Combo Box**. Choose **Next** when ready. The next dialog box will appear similar to the following:

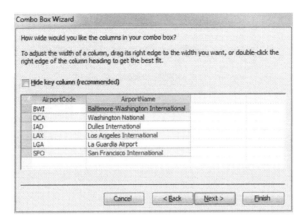

Step 8.   Adjust the display width of the column or columns that will appear in the **Combo Box** list. If working with two or more fields and one of the fields is a **Primary** Key, Access will default to **Hide key column**. For primary key fields that do not contain useful information (such as StaffID, or book ISBN) this is a good choice. Choose **Next**.

Step 9.   If you elected to not hide the **Primary Key** *or* your **Combo Box** will not use a **Primary Key** field, the following dialog box will appear. Use it to determine which field (selected in Steps 6 and 7) will serve to bind the **Combo Box** either to the **Control Source**, or to the control's **Value** property (depending upon the choice you make in the next step).

The next dialog box will appear similar to the following:

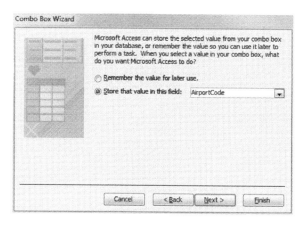

Step 10. Select whether the **Combo Box** will be unbound or bound. Use the following table as a guide. When ready, choose **Next**.

Option	Description
Remember the value for later use.	This creates an *unbound* **Combo Box**. The value displayed by the combo box is stored in the **Combo Box's** *Value* property. Exception: In combo boxes that display more than one field, the *bound column* property controls which field value is stored by the combo box's *value* property.
Store that value in this field:	This creates a *bound* **Combo Group**. Use the drop-down list to choose the field which will accept the **Combo Box's** *Value* property.

The final dialog box of the **Combo Box Wizard** will appear similar to the following:

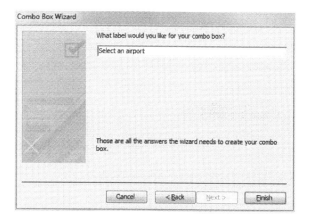

Step 11.   Type a name for the label of the **Combo Box**. Choose **Finish**. The **Combo Box** in **Form Design View** will appear similar to the following:

In the previous procedure two fields were chosen from a table named tblAirports. The first column is the binding column and the results are stored in a field bound to the form named *AirportCode*. The following table outlines the significant properties set by the Wizard to create this **Combo Box**.

Property	Value
Column Count	*2*
Column Widths	*1";1.8959"* (if you wish the first column to be hidden, set the first measure to 0
Control Source	*AirportCode* (a field name - if the control will be bound to an underlying field on the form. Otherwise this property would be blank if the control is to store the current selection as part of the *Value* property.
Row Source Type	*Table/Query*
Row Source	*SELECT [tblAirports].[AirportCode], [tblAirports].[AirportName] FROM [tblAirports];*

How to Use the Combo Box Wizard to Create a Custom List of Values

In this approach, you manually enter the values you wish to present to the user. This isn't as elegant an approach as the first example since you need to open the form in **Form Design View** if you need to make changes to your list, whereas a combo box bound to a lookup table is updated when you make changes to the lookup table data . Still, it helps greatly to reduce the incidence of data entry errors by enforcing the rule that users must select from the list of options.

Step 1.   Enable the **Control Wizard**.

Step 2.   Select the **Combo Box** control.

Step 3.   Draw a **Combo Box** onto the form.

Step 4.   In the first **Combo Box Wizard** dialog box, choose the second option, **I will type in the values that I want**. Choose **Next**. The second dialog box of the **Combo Box Wizard** will appear similar to the following:

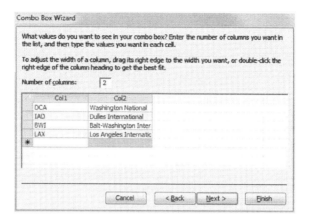

Step 5. In the **Number of columns** text box, type the number of columns you require, then move to the grid area of the dialog box and type the appropriate values you wish. When finished, choose **Next**.

Step 6. If you chose two or more columns in Step 5, the Wizard will ask you to choose the column to be used as the **Control Source**. In the illustration below the first column will bind the **Combo Box**. Select the appropriate column and select **Next**.

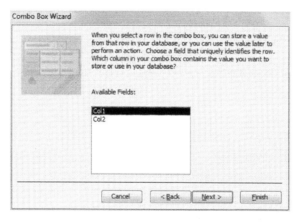

Step 7. Regardless of the number of columns you've created, the next dialog box determines whether you want to create a bound or unbound **Combo** Box. Use the following table as a guide. When ready, choose **Next**.

Option	Description
Remember the value for later use.	This creates an *unbound* **Combo Box**. The value displayed by the combo box is stored in the **Combo Box's** *Value* property. Exception: In combo boxes that display more than one field, the *bound column* property controls which field value is stored by the combo box's *value* property.
Store that value in this field:	This creates a *bound* **Combo Box**. Use the drop-down list to choose the field that will accept the **Combo Box's** *Value* property.

Step 8.   In the last dialog box of the **Combo Box Wizard**, type a name for the **Combo Box**. Choose **Finish.**

Considering the screen shots from the previous procedure, these are the significant properties set by the Wizard to create a **Combo Box** that uses a built-in list of 2 columns with the first column being the binding column:

Property	Value
Column Count	*2*
Column Widths	*1" ; 1"* (if you wish the first column to be hidden, set the first measure to 0
Control Source	*AirportCode* (a field name - if the control will be bound to an underlying field on the form. Otherwise this property would be blank if the control is to store the current selection as part of the *Value* property.
Row Source Type	*Value List*
Row Source	*"DCA";"Washington National Airport";"IAD";"Dulles International";"LAX";"Los Angeles International"*

How to Use the Combo Box Wizard to Find Records on the Form

When you select the wizard option to locate a specific record on a form, you are creating an unbound **Combo Box** control. Unlike the previous two situations, in this instance the wizard creates a VBA procedure to elicit the steps required to locate and display a specific record. You can use such a control as a *Quick Search* feature on your form.

You must be able to uniquely identify the records in some manner. Knowledge of the primary key for the underlying form record source is essential.

 Your form *must* be bound and have a *Primary Key* field associated with it in order for this option to be available via the **Combo** or **List Box** Wizard.

Step 1.   Enable the **Control Wizard**.

Step 2.   Select the **Combo Box** control.

Step 3.   Draw a **Combo Box** onto the form. The **Combo Box** Wizard will start.

Step 4.   Choose the third option, **Find a record on my form based on the value I selected in my combo box.** Choose **Next.** The second dialog box of the **Combo Box Wizard** will appear similar to the following:

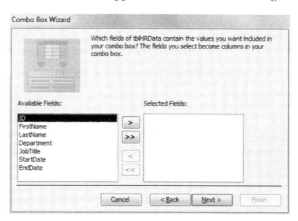

Step 5.   Use the **Add (>)** or the **Add all (>>)** button to add fields to the **Selected Fields** list. Note that it isn't necessary to include the **Primary** Key field - Access should deduce its presence and automatically include and hide that field on the **Combo** Box. Choose **Next**. The third dialog box of the **Combo Box Wizard** will appear similar to the following:

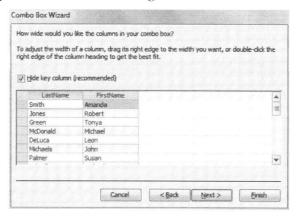

Step 6.   Adjust the width of the columns, if desired. Adjust the visibility of the **Primary Key** field, if desired. Choose **Next.**

Step 7.   In the final dialog box, type a label for the **Combo Box**.

Step 8.   Choose **Finish.**

The **Combo Box** properties that are set using this procedure are similar to those set when you create a combo box that looks up existing values (see page 90). The major difference with a **Combo Box** that locates a specific record is a macro procedure is placed in the control's **After Update** event procedure.

How to Manage Redundant Data in Combo and List Boxes

If you use a Wizard to create a lookup list for a **Combo** or **List** box it may display redundant data. For example, creating a list that looks up *Department* from an employees table will list the department *Management* as many times as there are staff in that table assigned to that department. This behavior isn't useful if your intent is to use a **Combo** or **List Box** to simplify data entry.

Because Wizards ultimately convert their actions into SQL (Structured Query Language) statements, you can add the SQL DISTINCT clause to the control's **Row Source** property.

Step 1.   Open the desired form in **Form Layout** or **Form Design** view and select the **Combo** or **List Box** you wish to adjust.

Step 2.   Open the **Property Sheet** for the control and move to the **Data** tab.

Step 3.   Select the text area associated with the **Row Source** property. The contents should include a SQL statement that begins with the clause SELECT.

Step 4.   Type the word DISTINCT *after* the SELECT clause. Ensure that there are spaces before and following DISTINCT.

Step 5.   Open the form in **Form** view and test the control.

You can also elicit this effect by using the **Builder** associated with the **Row Source** property to open the **Query Editor**. Click anywhere in the **Table** area but not on a table representation. Open the **Property Sheet** for the query and set the **Unique Values** property to *Yes*. Return to the form and save your changes.

Option Buttons, Toggle Buttons, and Check Boxes

These three controls are related in that an individual control can display one of two states: *Yes/On/True* or *No/Off/False*. They are typically used as bound controls to a field of the Yes/No data type. An alternative mode for each of these controls may be set by adjusting their **Triple State** property. When set to *Yes*, these controls pick up an additional state: *Null* (which is taken in most database applications to mean *I don't know*).

When working with one of these controls which is bound to a field of the Yes/No data type, you only need a single control for that field. The state of an **Option Button**, **Toggle Button**, and a **Check Box** - all bound to the same Yes/No field, is illustrated below. The upper illustration shows the controls signaling a Yes/True/On state. The lower illustration shows the controls in the No/False/Off state.

When you place two or more **Option Buttons**, **Toggle Buttons**, or **Check Boxes** on a form, the behavior depends upon whether they are part of an **Option Group**. If not, each control behaves independently of the other controls. In this context, you would use several copies of a control either bound to different fields of the Yes/No data type, or if unbound, to ask unrelated questions of the end user.

In the following illustration there are three instances of each control type. Each is bound to a separate field (there are 9) of the Yes/No data type. The controls behave independently of one another since they are displaying the field values for their respective bound fields.

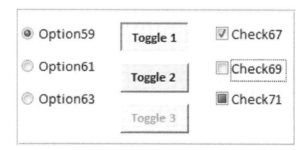

The controls illustrated above have their **Triple State** property set to *Yes*. In some Office Themes, the *Null* value for an **Option Button** does not display clearly so it is recommended that you use **Toggle Buttons** or **Check Boxes** if you need to display a third, *Null* state. For each control type illustrated above, the first control is indicating the Yes/True/On state. The second row of controls are bound to fields with the No/False/Off value. The lower row shows controls bound to field values of the *Null* value.

If you place two or more instances of the same control type within an **Option Group** the behavior changes from that illustrated above. The entire frame becomes the bound control and the **Option Buttons**, **Toggle Buttons**, or **Check Boxes** are configured to show a single field value from a list of possible values. If bound to a field of the Yes/No data type at most you can have three controls - mapping to each of three possible states: *Yes/True/On*, *No/False/Off*, and *Null*. If the **Option Group** is bound to a field of a Number data type, the number of controls possible within the group increases to match the total number of possible states in the field value. For example, if a Number field can contain up to five numeric values, that is the number of **Option Buttons, Toggle Buttons**, or **Check Boxes** you can have within an **Option Group**. In either case, the **Option Group** enforces a rule that only one control within the **Group** may be selected.

A simple example showing three separate **Option Groups**, one containing **Option Buttons**, the middle one displaying **Toggle Buttons**, and the right-most group showing **Check Boxes** is presented below. All three **Option Groups** are bound to the same field of the Yes/No data type.

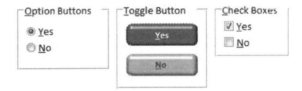

The same three groups, displaying the No/False/Off state would appear as:

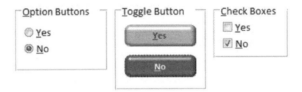

When working with three or more controls within an **Option Group**, it is a good practice to use the **Option Button** control type. From its earliest days as a graphical interface control, the **Option Button** (they were formerly called *Radio Buttons*) was expected to behave in a manner that only a single button could be selected at a time. This behavior mimicked the older-style radios in automobiles that were used to select a preset radio station. Pushing in one button forced an already-depressed button to pop outward. Users expect **Check Boxes** to permit multiple selections, and their use in that mode will be addressed when discussing their use as unbound controls.

An example of 4 **Option Buttons** in a **Option Group** and bound to a text field, *PreferredContactMethod* is illustrated below. This field is of the Number data type and stores the following values: 1=Office Phone, 2=Mobile Phone, 3=eMail, 4=Text Message.

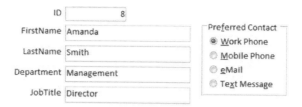

We will discuss working with these controls in four modes. First will be to work with a single bound control. Afterwards we will tour the **Option Group Wizard** to create multiple controls, each associated with a single value and all bound via the group to a single field. We will then create an **Option Group** manually. Lastly we will discuss using these controls in an unbound mode.

How to Manually Configure a Bound Option Button

This process is nearly identical for **Toggle Buttons** and **Check Boxes**. Ideally, you use a single bound **Option Button**, **Toggle Button**, or **Check Box** for each field of the Yes/No data type.

Step 1.   From the **Controls** group of the **Design** tab, select **Option Button**.

Step 2.   Draw the control on the form.

Step 3.   Adjust the control properties using the **Property Sheet**. See the following table for details.

The alternative method for creating an **Option Button, Toggle Button,** or **Check Box** is to draw a field of the Yes/No data type from the **Field List** onto the form. The default control will be a **Check Box**. If desired, right-click on the control and choose **Change to.** Changing control types is discussed on page 80.

Option Button, Toggle Button, and Check Box Properties

Property	Description
Control Source	The field the control is bound to.
Triple State	Determines whether the field can display a third state: *Null*. This option only applies to fields of the Yes/No data type. The default is *No*.
Use Theme	Only applies to **Toggle Buttons**. Determines whether a Microsoft Office Theme will apply to the control's appearance.

How to Use the Option Group Control Wizard

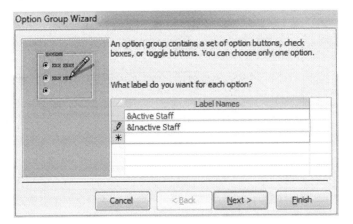

The **Option Group Wizard** simplifies the process of placing two or more **Option Buttons**, **Toggle Buttons**, or **Check Boxes** on a form. When placed within an **Option Group**, the controls are no longer capable of being bound to a field. Rather, the **Option Group** as a parent control manages the binding to a field. An **Option Group** may only be bound to fields of the Yes/No or Number data type.

When you create two or more controls for an **Option Group**, only one control may be selected at a time.

Step 1.   Enable the **Control Wizard**, located on the **Controls** group of the **Design** tab.

Step 2.   Select the **Option Group** control.

Step 3.   Draw an **Option Group** onto the form. The first dialog box of the **Option Group** wizard will appear similar to the following:

Step 4.   Enter two or more label names (these will correspond to the **Option Button, Toggle Button**, or **Check Box** labels). Choose **Next**. The second dialog box of the **Option Group Wizard** will appear similar to the following:

 Using the Ampersand character (&) in a label caption creates an *accelerator key*. Place the Ampersand immediately before the desired key. When the label caption is complete, the accelerator character will be indicated with an underscore.

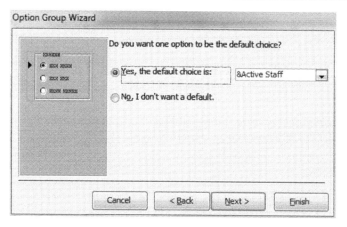

Step 5.   Select a **Default choice**, if desired. If the displayed label is not your default choice, select it from the drop-down list. Choose **Next**. The third dialog box of the **Option Group Wizard** will appear similar to the following:

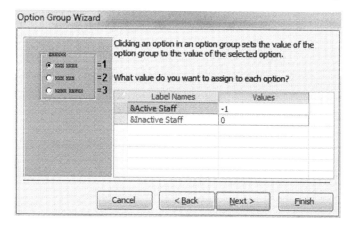

Step 6.   Assign numeric values to each of your option labels or accept the default values. If the bound field is of the Yes/No data type, you can type Yes/True/On or

No/False/Off in a cell in the **Values** column. Access will convert Yes to -1 and No to 0. Choose **Next**. The fourth dialog box of the **Option Group Wizard** will appear similar to the following:

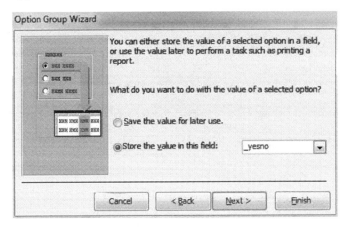

Step 7.   Select whether the **Option Group** will be unbound or bound. Use the following table as a guide. When ready, choose **Next**.

Option	Description
Save the value for later use.	Creates an *unbound* **Option Group**. The numeric value of the selected control (corresponding to the values indicated in Step 6) are stored in the **Option Group's** *Value* property.
Store the value in this field:	Creates a *bound* **Option Group**. Use the drop-down list to choose the field that will accept the **Option Group's** *Value* property. You may bind the **Option Group** to a field of either the Yes/No or Number data type.

The fifth dialog box of the **Option Group Wizard** will appear similar to the following:

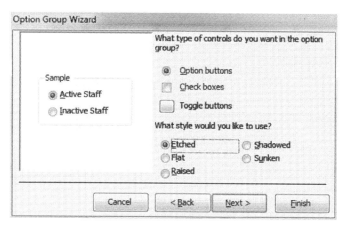

Step 8.   Select a **Control Type** and **Control Style** for your **Option Group**. Choose **Next**. The last dialog box of the **Option Group Wizard** will appear similar to the following:

Step 9.   Type a name for the **Option Group** caption. Choose **Finish**. The **Option Group** in **Form Design View** will appear similar to the following:

Important Option Group Properties

Property	Control	Description
Control Source	Option Group	Determines the *bound* field if the Option Group is acting as a *bound control*. This property should be blank if the Option Group is unbound.
Default Value	Option Group	Indicates which Option Button, Toggle Button, or Check Box is selected by default. The number corresponds to the Option Value property (see below).
Option Value	Option Button Toggle Button Check Box	Assigns a numeric value to each Option Button, Toggle Button, or Check Box control in the Option Group. When a particular control is selected, the Option Value is stored in the Option Group's *Value* property. Note that the *value* property is not available in the Property Sheet.

How to Manually Create an Option Group

The **Option Group** Wizard simplifies the task of creating a set of interrelated **Option Buttons**, **Toggle Buttons**, or **Check Boxes** by automating the property settings listed in the previous table. When you manually create an **Option Group**, you must draw the **Option Group** frame first and then draw the desired controls on the frame. As you conduct the latter step the background of the frame will darken - this is Access' way of verifying that the control will be part of your **Option Group**. If you create the **Option Buttons**, **Toggle Buttons**, or **Check Boxes** first and then draw the frame, the controls will not become part of the **Option Group**.

You must be in **Form Design View** to create this control.

Step 1.   If necessary, disable **Use Control Wizards**, located on the **Tools** group.

Step 2.   Select the **Option Group** control and draw an **Option Group** on your form.

Step 3.   Select either the **Option Buttons**, **Toggle Buttons**, or **Check Box** tool.

Step 4.   Draw the desired number of controls on top of the **Option Group**. The **Option Group** background should darken as you add each control.

Step 5.   For each control you've placed on the **Option Group**, adjust the control's **Caption** property (you can directly edit the control's attached label or use the **Property Sheet**).

Step 6.   Open the **Property Sheet** and move to the **Data** tab. For each control on the **Option Group**, modify the **Option Value** property. The value you enter for each control must be a number (for Yes/True/On and No/False/Off settings you can enter *Yes* and *No*, respectively. Recall that the **Option Value** will specify the value to be associated with the **Option Group** control source property. See the previous table for discussion.

Step 7. Select the **Option Group** and return to the **Property Sheet**. If the **Option Group** is to be bound, choose a field from the drop down box associated with the **Control Source** property. If the control is to be unbound, leave this property blank. Recall that unbound **Option Group** controls store the **Option Value** as the *value* property.

How to Manually Configure an Unbound Option Button

When you place two or more **Option Buttons**, **Toggle Buttons**, or **Check Boxes** on a form without containing them in an **Option Group**, they behave independently of one another. Users may expect **Option Buttons** and **Toggle Buttons** to interact, so the **Check Box** is a good choice for working with multiple, unbound controls within this family.

A good example of the use of **Check Box** controls that are unbound appears in the following illustration.

Step 1. Ensure that your form is either in **Form Layout** or **Form Design View.**

Step 2. Select the desired control type and place it on the form.

Step 3. Open the **Property Sheet** and move to the **Other** tab. Enter a name for the control in the **Name** text box.

 Providing a name for the control is useful since the control is unbound. Referring to it via an expression, a macro, or in VBA code will require addressing the control by name.

Using an Unbound Checkbox

Unbound **Check Box**, **Option Button**, and **Toggle Button** controls require macros or VBA programming in order to make them useful. Once unbound, they enter the realm of user interface controls and generally serve a different function than when bound.

As an example of using an unbound checkbox, we'll work through the functionality required to implement part of the previous illustration - the **Print** command button and the **Preview First** check box. We'll create a macro that will become attached to the *Click* event of the **Command Button** (these are discussed following the next section on **Subforms**). The macro will include an *If..Else* logic block that will manage either opening the report in **Print Preview** or sending it directly to the default printer - depending upon the value of the check box.

We will assume you have a form named *frmPrintSwitchboard* and a report named *rptBudget*.

Step 1.   Create a command button (discussed beginning on page 116) and name it *cmdPrintReport*.

Step 2.   Create a **Check Box** and name it *chkPrintPreview*

Step 3.   From the **Create** tab, in the **Macros & Code** area choose **Macro**. The **Macro Editor** will open.

Step 4.   In the **Drop Down Box**, select the **IF** macro action. The **Macro Editor** will appear similar to the following:

Step 5.   In the *Conditional expression* text box enter the following expression:

Forms![frmPrintSwitchBoard]![chkPrintPreview].value = true

You could have selected the **Builder** to assist with this expression by choosing the current database and drilling down to your *frmPrintPreview* form, then choosing one of the form's objects, *chkPrintPreview*. You would manually enter the *=True* text. In essence, this expression refers to whether the checkbox *chkPrintPreview* is checked (True) when the macro runs.

Step 6.   Choose the **Drop Down Box** associated with the **If** action and select *OpenReport*.

Step 7.   In the new text areas that appear, enter *rptBudget* in the **Report Name** text area and select *Print Preview* in the **View** area.

Step 8.   Select the **Add Else** hyperlink. In the **Add New Action** text area associated with the **Else** action, choose *Open Report*.

Step 9.   In the new text areas that appear, enter *rptBudget* in the **Report Name** text area and select *Print*. The **Macro Editor** at this point should appear similar to the following:

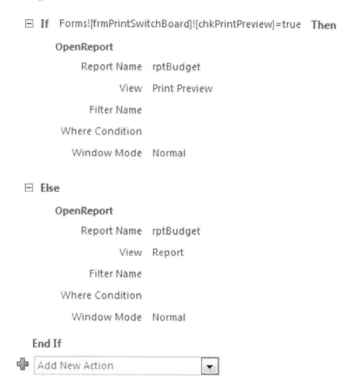

Step 10.   Save the macro using the name *macPrintBudget*.

Step 11.   Return to your form (in **Form Design View**) and open the **Property Sheet** for the *cmdPrintReport* **Command Button**.

Step 12.   Move to the **Events** tab and in the **Drop Down Box** associated with the *On Click* event, select the *macPrintBudget* macro.

This works because the macro is using an If..Else logic block. The test condition is whether the *chkPrintPreview* checkbox is checked (its value equals *True*). If checked, the initial part of the macro is run which opens the report in *Print Preview*. If not checked, the *Else* portion of the macro runs which opens the report by sending it directly to the printer.

Macros are one way to elicit this type of behavior. Another approach, which offers far greater control over how objects are automated is to use VBA code. There is a book in this series titled *Building VBA Apps Using Microsoft Access*.

Subform Control

This control mediates the interaction between data sets when tables are related in a one-to-one or a one-to-many relationship. As its name suggests, the control displays a subform that synchronizes the display of data - in this case the master or containing form is associated with data from the *one* side of the *one-to-many* relationship, or in the case of a *many-to-many* relationship the master form manages the data from the primary table of interest. The **Subform** contains a form that displays the synchronized data from the other side of the relationship join. The concept of *master* (main form) and *child* (subform) are useful here as two important properties, **Link Master Fields** and **Link Child Fields** are important mediators in the synchronization between these two objects.

Although it is possible to create a Form/Subform pair using tables that have not been formally joined using the **Relationships Window** it is a best practice to relate your tables by establishing joins *prior* to designing forms and reports. If you choose to create a Form/Subform pair using unjoined tables, you'll need to know in advance what field or fields in the two tables will serve as primary and foreign keys.

Like so many other controls, placing a **Subform Control** on a form using a Wizard greatly simplifies the process. Placing a **Subform** on a form using a **Control Wizard** will be addressed first, followed by discussion of working with this control type manually. Throughout these procedures we'll refer to the form contained within the **Subform** control as the *contained* form.

How to Use the Subform Control Wizard

The form that contains data from the *one* side of a *one-to-many* join, or contains the information of primary interest in a *many-to-many* join should be opened in **Form Design View.**

Step 1.   Ensure that **Use Control Wizards** is enabled, then select the **Subform/Subreport** control and draw the control on your form. The first dialog box of the **Subform** wizard will appear similar to the following:

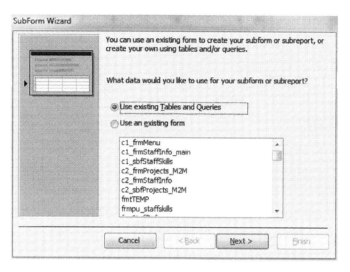

Step 2. Choose either an existing table/query or an existing form to embed in the new **Subform**, then select **Next**. If you selected an existing form, proceed to Step 4, otherwise selecting an existing table or query will open the following dialog box:

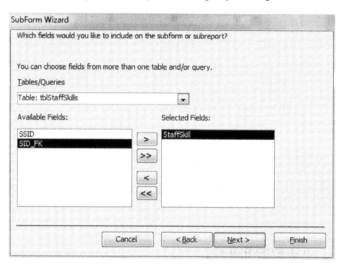

Step 3. Use the **Tables/Queries** drop down box to select the desired table. Once selected, add the desired fields from the **Available Fields** box to the **Selected Fields** box. (The > and >> controls add a single field or all fields, respectively). Select **Next**.

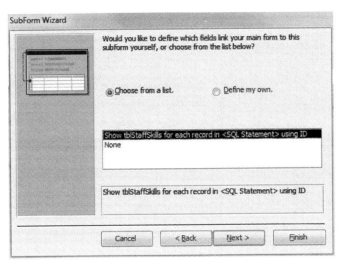

Step 4. If your tables were previously joined using the **Relationships Window**, Access will suggest the field or fields which will link the form and subform. If the suggested relationship is correct, choose **Next** and proceed to Step 6. If the relationship hasn't been established or you need to manually configure the linking fields, select **Define my own**. In this case the **Subform Wizard** will display the following dialog box:

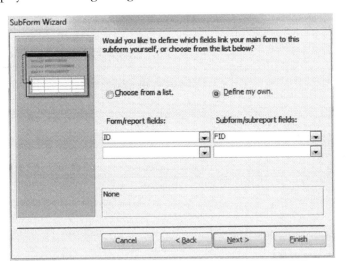

Step 5. Choose the primary key field or fields that are bound to the form in the **From/report fields** drop down box(es). Match these to the corresponding foreign key fields present in the record source for the **Subform** using the **Subform/subreport fields** drop down box(es). Choose **Next** when done.

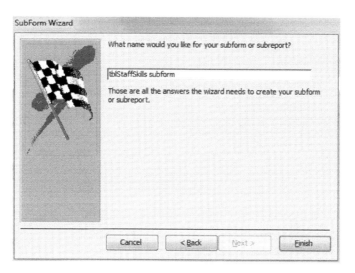

Step 6.   Type a name for the **Subform** control and choose **Finish**. The name you enter in this step will resolve to a named **Form** in the **Navigation Pane** area. The **Subform** and its **Master Form** will appear similar to the following in **Form Design View**:

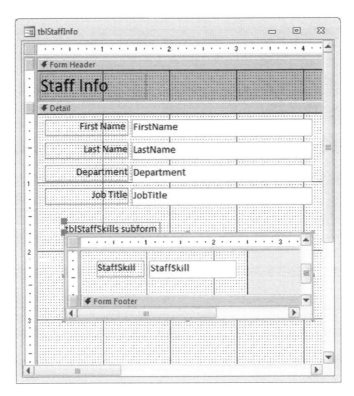

When you use the **Subform Wizard** to place a **Subform**, the following subform properties, all located on the **Data** tab in the **Property Sheet,** are modified.

Property	Description
Source Object	The name of the *contained* form within the **Subform** control. *All* contained forms exist as separately named form objects.
Link Master Fields	The field bound to the main or *Master* form that represents the *primary key*. If there are two or more fields that constitute the primary key their names are separated with semicolons (;).
Link Child Fields	The field from the contained form (the **Source Object** for the **Subform**) that serves as the *foreign key* field to the master form's primary key. If there are two or more fields their names are separated by semicolons.

How to Manually Create a Subform

When you use the **Subform Wizard** to create a subform, it will build the contained form even if it doesn't exist. When you manually create a **Subform**, the contained form must exist ahead of time.

Step 1.   Open the form which will serve as the **Master Form** in **Form Design View**.

Step 2.   Select the **Subform** control and draw it onto the **Master Form**.

Step 3.   Open the **Property Sheet** for the **Subform** control and move to the **Data** tab.

Step 4.   Choose the form which will be contained by the **Subform** from the list of forms in the **Source Object** drop down box.

Step 5.   Select the **Builder** in either the **Link Master Fields** or **Link Child Fields** text area. A dialog box similar to the following will appear:

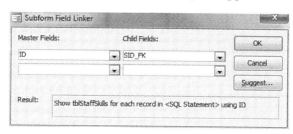

Step 6.   In the **Master Fields** area choose the field or fields which constitute the Primary Key on the **Master Form**.

Step 7.   In the **Child Fields** area choose the field or fields which constitute the Foreign Key on the form contained by the **Subform** control. Choose **OK**.

 You can also add a **Subform** by dragging a form from the **Navigation Pane** and placing on your **Master Form** opened in **Form Design View**. A **Subform** control is automatically created. Open the **Property Sheet** for the **Subform** and proceed with Step 3, above.

Points on Subform Controls

▪ The **Subform** control is separate from the **Form** it contains. To select the **Subform** click anywhere on the **Subform** object. If the mouse pointer is over the contained **Form** (i.e. the subform) and you click a second time, you will select an object on that form.

▪ You can make design changes to the contained **Subform** in one of three ways:

  o In **Form Design** View, click twice over the **Subform**. Move to the desired area of the contained form and make design changes as desired.

  o In **Form Design** View, right-click on the **Subform** border and choose **Subform in New Window** from the short cut menu. The contained form will appear in a separate **Form Design** window.

- o With the **Master Form** closed, open the contained form that serves as the **Source Object** for the **Subform** and move to **Form Design View**. Make design changes as desired.

- Frequently the **Subform Wizard** will create a contained form that is unusually wide. You may need to resize the controls on the contained form first, then decrease the width of the contained form, followed by adjusting the width or height of the **Subform**.

- If the contained **Form** is larger than the **Subform** (think of the latter as being a viewport to the contained **Form**), one or both scrollbars will appear when the **Master Form** is viewed either in **Form Layout** or **Form Design View**. In **Form Layout** view you can adjust either the dimensions of the contained form or the **Subform** so that the scroll bars disappear.

 The latter point is an important design goal. **Subforms** make a regular form complicated enough - for example the user now interacts with an additional **Navigation Control**. Removing scrollbars helps keep your form interface clean and free of clutter.

Command Button

A **Command Button** is an unbound control that elicits some action when selected. You interact with command buttons every day in all graphical operating systems. Working with a **Command Button** without using a **Control Wizard** requires knowledge of macros or VBA coding. In former versions of Access, using a **Control Wizard** when placing a **Command Button** on a form generated VBA programming code. In Access 2010 the default is to generate an embedded **Macro**. Macro code may be converted to VBA code in Access 2010.

Adding a **Command Button** using a Wizard is the easiest approach, so we'll discuss it first. Creating a **Command Button** manually does require some knowledge of either macros or VBA programming. We'll briefly address that approach as well.

Points on Command Buttons

- A **Command Button** can display a caption, an image, or both. When using an image without a caption ensure that the graphic clearly defines the **Command Button** function.

- **Command Buttons** *must* have an attached macro or VBA procedure - otherwise their presence on a form is meaningless. Unless you are versed in creating macros or VBA procedures, use the **Command Button Wizard** to automate macro or VBA code production.

- In Access 2010 the **Command Button Wizard** creates an *embedded* macro. It will not appear in the **Macro** group on the **Navigation Pane**. You can create a **Macro** ahead of creating the **Command Button** and manually attach your **Macro** to the **Command Button's** *On Click* event.

- An embedded macro can be converted into VBA code. In this case the code is placed in the *Click* event handler.

 A best practice is to always place a **Cancel** and a **Close** command button on each data entry form, and if you create a main menu, a **Quit** button. Good interface design dictates that these controls are always placed in a consistent location between forms.

How to Use the Command Button Wizard - General Procedure

You can be in either **Form Layout** or **Form Design View** when using this wizard. This procedure will outline the basic steps to create a **Command Button**. The following procedure will detail how to use the **Command Button Wizard** to open a form.

Step 1.   Ensure that **Use Control Wizards** is enabled, then select the **Command Button** control and draw a rectangle on your form. The first dialog box of the **Command Button Wizard** will appear similar to the following:

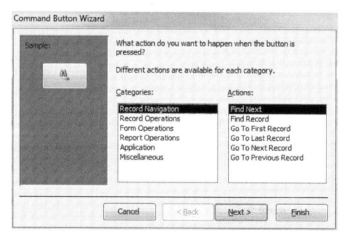

Step 2.   Select a **Category** and then select an **Action**. Use the following table as a guide.

Category	Description
Record Navigation	Find a record, find the next record, or move to the first, last, next or previous record.
Record Operations	Add, delete, print, duplicate, save a record or undo data entry.
Form Operations	Open or print a form, apply a filter, refresh form data.
Report Operations	Open, print, email a report or save it to a file.
Application	Quit Access.
Miscellaneous	Start the *auto dialer*, print a table, run a macro or a query.

Step 3   If you choose an action that works on a specific object (for example to open a form, print a report, or run a query), a dialog box similar to the following will appear: Choose the target object and select **Next.**

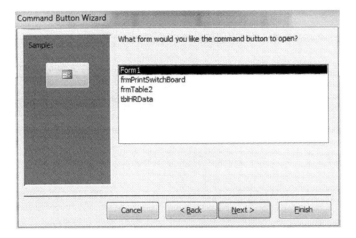

Step 4.   If you wish to open a **Form** see the following procedure for details. Otherwise for all other procedures the following dialog box will appear. Choose whether to use **Text** or a **Picture** for your **Command Button** (other settings are discussed following this procedure). Choose **Next** when done.

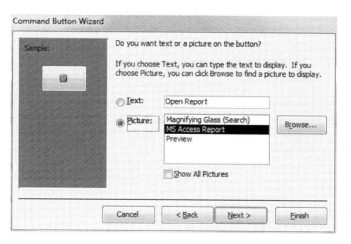

Step 5.   In the last dialog box, enter a name for your **Command Button** and choose **Finish.**

Important Command Button Properties

Property	Description
Caption	Specifies the caption text for the **Command Button**.
Picture Caption Arrangement	Controls whether a caption and an image share the **Command Button** interface. If both are present, predefined properties dictate where the caption appears in relation to the picture.
Picture Type	Controls whether the picture is *Embedded*, *Linked*, or *Shared*. If you attach a custom button image, *Embedded* (the default) is preferred because you can distribute copies of the form without worrying about distributing the graphic file as well. Linked pictures refer to an image stored on the local computer or a common network share. A Shared image has been previously loaded using the **Insert Image** tool.
Picture	Sets the image file (bitmap or icon) used for the **Command Button's** picture. The *Picture* property takes precedence over the *Caption* property, thus if both properties have values, the picture will appear on the **Command Button**.
Use Theme	Controls whether the appearance of the **Command Button** is aligned with the current Microsoft Office Theme.
On Click	The *event procedure* that contains the VBA code used to implement the **Command Button's** action.
Name	Sets the name of the control. The *Name* property is used also to name all the *event procedures* for the **Command Button**.
Default	Determines if the **Command Button** is activated when the user presses the *Enter* key. Only one **Command Button** on a form may have this property set to *Yes*.

How to Use the Command Button Wizard - Opening Forms

When you use the **Command Button Wizard** to open a **Form**, there are additional options presented which are not part of the generalized procedure for using this Wizard. You can choose to open a form that displays all records (e.g. it is not filtered), or open a form that displays filtered results. In the latter case, the filtering depends upon the two forms (the master containing the **Command Button** and the child containing the filtered records) being related in a *one-to-many* relationship. If this isn't the case do not choose that option when asked.

Step 1.   Follow the previous procedure for Steps 1 and 2. When the dialog box requests an action category, choose **Form Operations** and select **Open a Form** from the list of options.

Step 2.   Choose the form to open from the list presented by the **Command Button Wizard**. Choose **Next**. The third dialog box of the Wizard will appear similar to the following:

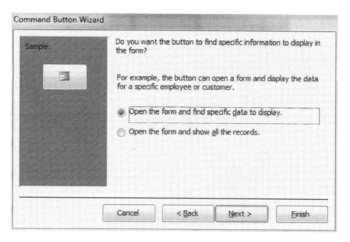

Step 3. To simply open the form, select **Open the form and show all the records**. If you choose this option, skip to Step 5. If you wish to open the form and restrict the records, select **Open the form and find specific data to display**. In this case, choose **Next** and proceed with the next step.

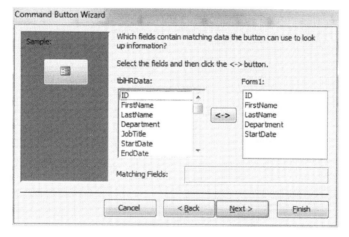

Step 4. Select the fields that link the current form to the form you wish to open. With this option, you are creating a *linked* form, which was introduced on page 18. In most cases, you should choose the Primary Key field from the left-hand list and the foreign key field from the right-hand list. Choose **Next** when done.

Step 5. Choose whether to use **Text** or a **Picture** for the **Command Button** label. This option is the same as Step 4 from the previous procedure. Choose **Next** when ready.

Step 6. Provide a name for the new **Command Button**, then choose **Finish.**

How to Manually Create a Command Button and Attach an Existing Macro

You create a **Macro** by opening the **Macro Editor** (**Create** tab, **Macros & Code** group, **Macro** command). You should create the **Macro** prior to using this procedure. Macros are discussed in Appendix B.

Step 1.   Ensure that **Use Control Wizards** is disabled.

Step 2.   Select the **Command Button** control and draw a rectangle on the **Form**.

Step 3.   Open the **Property Sheet** for the **Command Button** and move to the **Event** tab.

Step 4.   Use the **Drop Down Box** associated with the **On Click** property to select the desired **Macro.**

How to Manually Create a Command Button and Attach a VBA Procedure

This is the way the **Command Button Wizard** created functionality in previous versions of Access. Use this procedure if you understand VBA programming. The following procedure discusses how to convert an embedded macro into a VBA code fragment.

Step 1.   Ensure that **Use Control Wizards** is disabled.

Step 2.   Select the **Command Button** control and draw a rectangle on the **Form**.

Step 3.   Open the **Property Sheet** for the **Command Button** and move to the **Event** tab.

Step 4.   Use the **Drop Down Box** associated with the **On Click** property and choose **[Event Procedure]**.

Step 5.   Select the **Builder (...)** associated with the **On Click** property. The **VBA Code Editor** will open and place you in the **Command Button's** *Click* event handler.

Step 6.   Construct your VBA code within this procedure. Close the **VBA Code Editor** when finished. This will return you to the **Form Design View** in Access.

How to Convert an Embedded Macro to VBA Code

If you're familiar with the VBA created by the **Command Button Wizard** in earlier versions of Access, you can convert the embedded macro created by the Wizard in Access 2010 to VBA Code. This procedure *will not work* with **Macros** generated by the **Macro Editor**, only with the macros generated by the **Command Button Wizard**. Note that this procedure will convert *all* embedded macros on the current **Form.**

Step 1.   Open the desired **Form** in **Form Design View**.

Step 2.   On the **Design** tab, in the **Tools** group, choose **Convert Form's Macros to Visual Basic**. A dialog box similar to the following will appear:

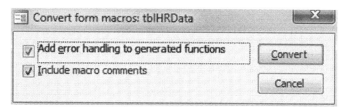

Step 3.   Modify the default conversion settings if desired. Error handling is recommended. Access stores macros as XML. Including **macro comments** will place the XML version of the **Macro** as commented lines in the VBA procedure. Choose **Convert** when done.

For each embedded **Macro** on the form, Access will create VBA code in the appropriate event handler. You can jump to the desired code fragment by selecting the **Property Sheet** for the desired control, and on the **Event** tab, choose the **Builder (...)** associated with the *On Click* event.

Line and Rectangle Controls

 These two controls are stylistically and functionally related. Unlike the controls discussed so far, the only purpose of these unbound controls is to provide some organization to your form. Although both controls are always unbound, the **Rectangle Control** is capable of recognizing some mouse-based events which can be used to elicit action via a **Macro** or a VBA procedure. The creation of **Lines** and **Rectangles** is a manual process - there are no associated control wizards for these controls.

Points on Line and Rectangle Controls

▪ The **Line** control may exist in any orientation (horizontal, vertical or diagonally). Its best appearance is when it is in a horizontal or vertical orientation. If you have trouble placing the control to be exactly horizontal or exactly vertical adjust the control's **Height** or **Width** property to zero, respectively.

▪ The **Rectangle Control** always resides on the **Form** oriented parallel to the **Form's** borders. Diagonal and/or non-right angle corners are not possible.

- The default **Format** properties for a **Line** make the line appear flat and solid. A **Rectangle's** defaults make the control appear *etched* like an **Option Group**. Some of the **Format** properties that affect appearance are presented in a table at the end of this section. You can also use the **Format Painter** to quickly transfer border and background styles between controls.

- Although both controls serve to organize areas of a form, the **Rectangle Control** is frequently used to group related controls.

An example of a form which uses a **Line** and two **Rectangle Controls** to separate areas is illustrated below. The **Line** separates two broad areas that constitute the data fields about staff. The two **Rectangle Controls** enclose other controls not associated with data entry.

How to Create a Line or Rectangle

Line and **Rectangle Controls** are only available when your form is open in **Form Design View**.

Step 1. Select the **Line** or **Rectangle Control** from the **Controls** group.

Step 2. Move the mouse pointer to a location on your form that constitutes the beginning of the **Line** or **Rectangle**. Click and hold down the left mouse button.

Step 3. Use the mouse to draw out the extent of the **Line** or **Rectangle Control**. Release the mouse button when done.

Common Line and Rectangle Format Properties

Property	Description
Back Style	*Transparent* (default), or *Normal*. Normal controls a solid color.
Back Color	If **Back Style** is set to *Normal*, this property specifies the background color. See the note following this table for additional points.
Border Style	Controls the line style. This works in conjunction with the **Special Effect** property although the latter may override some **Border Style** settings.
Border Width	Controls line width. The default is *Hairline*, otherwise specify width in *points*.
Border Color	Controls line color. Choose from *Themed* colors or select the **Builder (...)** to choose from a color pallet.
Special Effect	These predefined settings provide an interesting set of styles - for example the default for an **Option Group** is *Etched*.

> If you apply a *Normal* **Back Style** to a **Rectangle Control** and the controls contained within disappear, you need to change the *z-order* for the **Rectangle**. Select it, then from the **Arrange** tab, in the **Sizing & Ordering** group, select **Send to Back**.

Tab Control

Like the **Line** and **Rectangle Controls**, the **Tab Control** assists in the organization of a **Form**. Tabbed forms and dialog boxes have been a regular feature of all operating systems for some time now. Indeed, in Access the **Property Sheet** is a classic example of a **Tab Control**. The **Tab Control** contains and arranges one or more **Page Controls** which each display a captioned tab. A **Page Control** is always associated with a **Tab Control** as it is an integral part of it, but is never associated outside the confines of the **Tab Control**. Neither the parent **Tab Control** or its containing **Page Controls** are bound, although it is common to place bound controls on a **Page**.

Tab Controls are very useful in organizing fields into related groups. Their adoption by many operating systems is testament to their usefulness.

Points on Tab Controls

- The **Tab Control** serves as a container for one or more **Pages**. Each **Page** acts as a container for bound and unbound controls. **Pages** can contain any other control *except* other

Tab Controls. For forms that require several **Subforms**, organizing them within a **Tab Control** is a useful technique that avoids cluttering the master form.

- When you place a **Tab Control** by default two **Pages** are added. Right clicking on a **Tab Control** opens a short cut menu that offers options for adding, deleting, or reordering **Pages**.

- A best practice is to add a **Tab Control** to a form *before* the bound controls are added. Although you can add a **Tab Control** *after* bound controls are in place, it is much easier to add controls to an existing **Page**. Working with **Tab Controls** once other controls are already in place is addressed as a procedure in this section.

- The **Format** properties for the **Tab Control** set properties that influence the overall border and the color of unselected **Pages** (basically their *tab* appearance). The tab caption is a property of a **Page**, but its formatting attributes are properties of the **Tab Control** and not the **Page.** This is to enforce a consistent look across all tabs within the control.

An example of a **Form** utilizing a **Tab Control** with **Pages** is illustrated below.

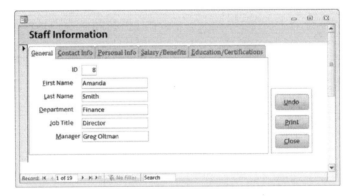

How to Add a Tab Control to a Form

Working with **Tab Controls** is more straightforward when you are in **Form Design View**.

Step 1.   From the **Controls** group elect the **Tab Control.**

Step 2.   Draw the **Tab Control** onto the form. The **Tab Control** in **Form Design View** will appear similar to the following:

Step 3.   Adjust any properties using the **Property Sheet**, as desired.

Common Tab Control Properties

Property	Description
Multi Row	Determines whether the **Tab Control** can display multiple rows of tabs. The default is *No*.
Tab Fixed Width/Height	Forces a specific width and/or height to the tabs. The default is zero, which allows the width of each tab to vary depending upon the length of each **Page's** caption property.
Back Color	Controls the color of all unselected tabs.
Pressed Color	For the selected tab, sets the color for both the tab and the **Page**.
Font (various)	Sets the font attributes (font name, size, color, weight, etc.) for the text on each tab. The actual text is dictated by the **Caption** property of each **Page**.

How to Select the Tab Control

When you insert a **Tab Control** it becomes selected. The previous image shows the **Tab Control** as the selected object.

Step 1.   Click on the border for the **Tab Control.** It is helpful to keep the mouse away from the **Page** tabs to ensure that the **Tab Control** becomes selected.

 You can also select a **Tab Control** using the **Property Sheet**. Use the **Selection Type** drop down box to choose the **Tab Control** by name.

How to Select a Page on the Tab Control

In order to place other controls on a **Page**, you must first select the target **Page**.

Step 1.   Click on the desired **Page** tab. When a **Page** on the **Tab Control** is selected, it will appear similar to the following (**Page 2** is the selected object):

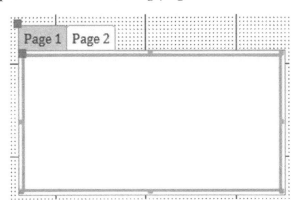

Important Tab Control Page Properties

Option	Description
Caption	Specifies the caption text for the tab.
Picture	Sets an image file (bitmap or icon) that can be displayed on the tab. Unlike **Command Buttons,** you cannot specify the layout between image and text. The image on a Tab always appears to the left of the caption.
Picture Type	Controls whether the picture is *Embedded* or *Linked*. If you attach a custom button image, *Embedded* (the default) is preferred because you can distribute copies of the form without worrying about distributing the BMP or ICO file too.
Page Index	Controls the order in which the pages appear in the **Tab Control**. The left-most **Page** has a **Page Index** property of 0.

How to Add Controls to a Page

The **Tab Control** only acts as a container for page controls. Thus, it is important that you select the page destined to be the target for any control you add. If, rather than a specific page, the **Tab Control** itself is selected, then the top-most page receives the new control.

Step 1.   Select the desired **Page** on the **Tab Control**.

Step 2.   Select the desired control from the **Controls** group and draw it into the **Page** or drag a bound field from the **Field List** onto the **Page**.

You cannot drag existing controls from elsewhere on the form onto a page (the dragged control will float above all **Pages** on the **Tab Control**). If you need to include an existing control, select it and **Cut** the control from the form, then select the page and **Paste** the control.

Tab Controls may accept any other control type except another **Tab Control**. Although they can accept **Page Break** controls, their use on a **Tab Control** is not typical as forms with **Tab Controls** only print the topmost **Page** from the control.

How to Add Pages to a Tab Control

You cannot control the order in which a new **Page** is added. Access always places the new page after any other **Pages**.

Step 1.   Select either the **Tab Control** or a **Page** on the control.

Step 2.   Right-click over the control and select **Insert Page** from the shortcut menu.

How to Remove a Page from a Tab Control

Step 1.   Select the **Page** you wish to remove.

Step 2.   Right-click on the **Page** and choose **Remove Page** from the shortcut menu, or press the *Delete* key.

How to Change the Page Order on a Tab Control

Step 1.   Right-click on the **Tab Control** or a **Page** on the control.

Step 2.   Select **Page Order** from the shortcut menu. A dialog box similar to the following will appear:

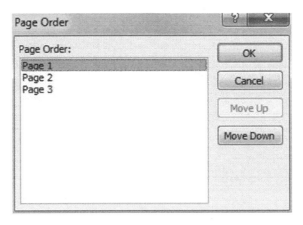

Step 3.　　In the **Page Order** list, select the **Page** to move.

Step 4.　　Use the **Move Up** or **Move Down** buttons to change the **Page** position.

Step 5.　　Choose **OK**.

> You can also change **Page** order by editing the **Page Index** property for a **Page**. Access will renumber the **Page Index** property of the other **Pages** on the control. **Page** numbering is *zero based* so the index of the left-most **Page** is zero and the right-most **Page** is one minus the number of **Pages**.

Navigation Control

This control serves a similar function to the **Tab Control** in that it organizes a form into separate units. Like a **Tab Control** the **Navigation Control** can arrange tabs that contain **Subform** or **Subreport** controls. The similarity ends there however. The **Navigation Control** differs in many respects from a **Tab Control**. For example:

- A **Navigation Control** can manage a secondary level of menu items - much like popular web pages that display a main navigation banner where each choice presents a secondary menu of options. Although the **Tab Control** can display multiple rows of tabs, nesting tab controls within a page isn't possible. The **Navigation Control** can only display two hierarchical levels corresponding to a main and subsidiary menu system.

- A **Navigation Control** consists of one or more **Navigation Buttons** and a **Navigation Subform**. A **Navigation Control** may only contain other forms or reports. In this capacity they serve well to manage top-level objects in a database application. **Tab Controls** can contain every other control type except other **Tab Controls**.

Because of the interplay between a **Navigation Control**, **Navigation Buttons**, and a **Navigation Subform** control, it is far easier to generate a **Navigation Control** by beginning with a **Navigation Form**. We'll step through creating a form this way and then explore the important properties to manage **Navigation Controls**.

How to Create a Navigation Form

Once the form has been created, it is opened in **Form Layout View**. This is a good starting point for naming the navigation tabs by dragging desired forms and reports onto the control.

Step 1.   Move to the **Create** tab and in the **Forms** group, choose **Navigation**. The control will display the following options:

Option	Description
Horizontal Tabs	Single level main menu with menu options arranged across the top of the **Navigation Control**. Each menu options is a separate **Navigation Button Control**.
Vertical Tabs, Left	Single level main menu, menu options (**Navigation Buttons**) arranged vertically along the left.
Vertical Tabs, Right	As above but menu options arranged vertically along the right.
Horizontal Tabs, 2 Levels	A two level menu system. The upper row becomes the *Main Menu* and the lower row is the *Subsidiary Menu*. The lower row is a separate **Navigation Control**. All menu options at both levels constitute separate **Navigation Buttons**.
Horizontal Tabs and Vertical Tabs, Left	As above except the *Subsidiary Menu* is located along the left side.
Horizontal Tabs and Vertical Tabs, Right	As above except the *Subsidiary Menu* is located along the right side.

Step 2.   Choose the desired **Navigation Form** style. A blank form will appear with the selected **Navigation Control** in **Form Layout View**.

How to Work with a Single Level Navigation Control

If you choose to work with any of the first three options from the previous table, your **Navigation Form** will manage a single level menu. For this type of control you first drag the desired form or report onto the control and then caption the **Navigation Buttons**.

You must be in **Form Layout View** to build a **Navigation Control** using drag and drop.

Step 1.   Create a **Navigation Form** using one of the first three options from the previous table. In the following illustration, a form of the **Horizontal Tab** type appears in **Form Layout View**.

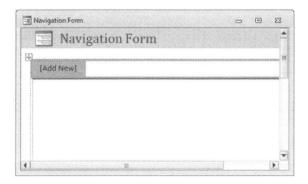

Step 2.   Drag an existing **Form** or **Report** from the **Navigation Pane** area and drop it onto the **[Add New]** tab.

Step 3.   The **Navigation Button** caption will show the name of the **Form** or **Report** just dropped. If desired, select the button by clicking once on it (you may need to click twice) to enter edit mode. Change the button caption by typing a new caption.

Step 4.   Repeat Steps 2 and 3 until you have added all the desired forms and reports to the **Navigation Control**.

The **Navigation Buttons** may be rearranged while in **Form Layout View**. Simply use the mouse to click and drag a **Navigation Button** to a new location.

How to Delete a Navigation Button

Deleting the button also removes the form or report associated with that button. The form or report isn't deleted - it is simply removed from the **Navigation Control**.

Step 1.   Open the form in **Form Layout** or **Form Design View**.

Step 2.   Select the desired **Navigation Button**.

Step 3.   Press the *Delete* key.

How to Work with a Two Level Navigation Control

The last 3 **Navigation Controls** presented in the table on page 131 are two level menu systems. The main menu will be the top-most or the only horizontal control. You will not drop forms or reports on the top level control - rather you will provide top-level captions to this control. For each top-level **Navigation Button** that is selected, you then drop forms or reports onto the second-level **Navigation Control**.

Step 1.   Create a **Navigation Form** using one of the last three options from the table on page 131. In the following illustration, a form of the **Horizontal Tabs, 2 Levels** type appears in **Form Layout View**.

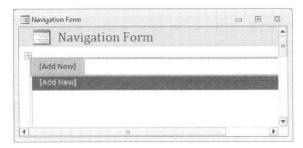

Step 2.   Select the top-most **[Add New]** control and type a caption appropriate for a top-level menu.

Step 3.   Drag a form or report to the lower **[Add New]** control. For left or right-oriented second-level **Navigation Controls**, this **[Add New]** button will be to the left or right of the **Navigation Subform**, respectively.

Step 4.   If desired, adjust the caption of the second-level **Navigation Button**.

Step 5.   For any other forms or reports which will appear grouped under the current top-level **Navigation Button**, repeat Steps 3 and 4.

Step 6.   When you are ready to create the next top-level **Navigation Button**, select the top-most **[Add New]** control. Type a caption appropriate for a top-level menu.

Step 7.   Repeat Steps 3-5 for the forms or reports you wish to group under the current top-level **Navigation Button**.

Step 8.   Repeat Steps 6 and 7 until all top level and all associated second level controls have been created. An example of a simple two menu form is illustrated below.

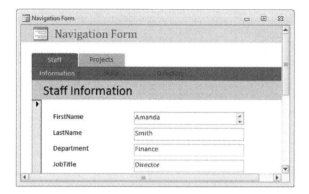

The current form displayed in the previous illustration is associated with the **Staff** top level menu and the **Information** second level menu. If the **Skills** menu was chosen the form would appear as follows:

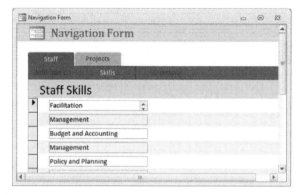

Whereas choosing the **Projects** top level menu would cause the **Navigation Form** to appear as:

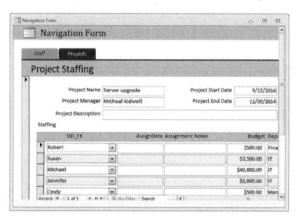

How to Work with a Navigation Control in Form Design View

It's easiest to design these controls in **Form Layout View**. However, some properties of these controls and the component parts are only available in **Form Design View**.

Step 1.   Open the form in **Form Design View**.

Step 2.   Select the desired element (it may be easier to select it by choosing the target control from the **Property Sheet Selection Type** drop down box).

Step 3.   Adjust properties as desired. The following tables list common properties.

Control	Property	Description
Navigation Control	**Span**	Determines whether the control is aligned horizontally or vertically.
Navigation Button	**Caption**	Sets the display text on the **Navigation Button**.
	Picture Caption Arrangement	Controls where the caption appears in relation to the picture, if the **Navigation Button** displays an image.
	Picture	The name of the picture to appear on the **Navigation Button**. Leave blank if no picture is to be displayed.
	Navigation Target Name	This is the name of the form or report which is linked to the **Navigation Button**. This object will appear in the **Navigation Subform** when the **Navigation Button** is selected. This property is *blank* if the **Navigation Button** is a member of a top-level menu when working with two-level **Navigation Forms**.
Navigation Subform	**Border Style, Width**	Sets the appearance of the edge of the **Navigation Subform**.

Bound and Unbound Object Frames

These controls specialize in presenting *OLE* (Object Linking and Embedding) data, either from a table (the bound control) or from a source unrelated to the containing form's record source. This is a technology that is part of the Windows operating system and permits users to not only view rich data but to edit or change it as well. When an OLE object, for example, a Microsoft Excel workbook, is embedded in either a bound or unbound object frame, double-clicking on the frame opens an instance of Microsoft Excel and displays the underlying data. The user can make changes to the worksheet and once closed, the changes are saved.

OLE allows a database to store data beyond the standard data types associated with a table field. For example, using OLE you can store staff images, Word documents that relate to a patent application, or an Excel workbook that contains project budget data. In fact, a single field of the **OLE** data type can house different forms of data on a record-by-record basis. The OLE data type is not supported by all database applications.

An unbound **Object Frame** would be used to add rich data to a form, but for the relatively unlikely scenario that it isn't connected to an underlying record set *yet* you would like end users to be able to edit the data contained within the frame.

The data types supported by the bound and unbound **Object Frames** are also supported by the **Attachment Control**, which is a newer addition to the list of Microsoft Access data types.

How to Add a Bound Object Frame to a Form

The form must have a field associated with its record source that is of the OLE data type. This control is only available when the form is in **Form Design View**.

Step 1.   From the **Field List** for the bound form, select the desired field of the OLE data type and drag it onto the form.

Step 2.   Size or move the control as needed.

 If the OLE data is associated with a registered object type, typically the data will display as if it were contained within the parent application. For example, an Excel worksheet will display as a small window looking into an Excel application. If the data are not of a registered object type, double clicking on the **Bound Object Frame** will open an application that Windows determines is the best app to view and/or edit the data.

 The alternative procedure would be to add a **Bound Object Frame** from the **Controls** group and then set its **Data** properties to bind it to an appropriate field from the form's record set.

How to Add an Unbound Object Frame to a Form

As mentioned in the introduction to **Object Frames**, this control may also display OLE data from a source outside of the database. An **Unbound Object Frame** will evoke a builder to select the external data the frame will contain. This occurs regardless of the status of the **Use Control Wizards** setting. This control is only available when the form is in **Form Design View**.

Step 1.   From the **Controls** group, select the **Unbound Object Frame**.

Step 2   Draw a rectangle on the form. The **Insert Object** builder will appear similar to the following:

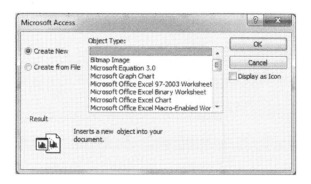

Option	Description
Create New	Select the appropriate application from the **Object Type** list. The application will open and you will create the data from scratch.
Create from File	Choose an existing file. An additional option, **Link** will appear. A *Linked* file can be independently edited in its parent application and Access will display the most recent changes. Otherwise the data are *embedded* and will only change if the parent application is evoked from within Access.
Display as Icon	For registered applications (e.g. those that are in the **Object Type** list, display an icon rather than a small view of the registered application with the data. Example: display an Microsoft Excel icon rather than a Microsoft Excel worksheet.

Step 3.   Choose to create new data, selecting from the list of registered applications. For example, you would choose **Bitmap Image** to generate and insert an image or **Microsoft Office Excel Workbook** to create a bound workbook object. If you choose this option proceed to Step 5. If you choose the **Create from File** the dialog box will appear similar to the following. Proceed to the next step in this procedure.

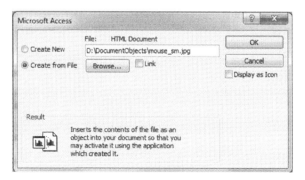

Step 4.   Browse to the appropriate location and select the file to embed. If you choose **Link**, and external changes to the file (example: an Excel Workbook that is

shared and edited by others) will update in Access. Choose **OK** when done. This completes this procedure.

Step 5.   If you chose to create the object new, the application you selected in Step 3 will automatically start and appear. For example, if you select **Bitmap Image**, Microsoft **Paint** will open. Create or load an image. An example of an image loaded into **Paint** appears below.

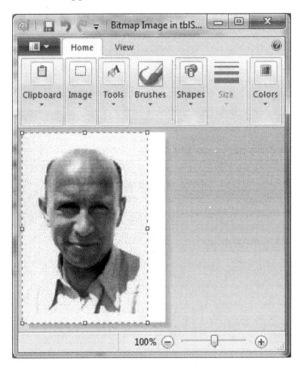

Step 6.   When your new data are ready, from the application managing the data select **Close and Return to Document** (the exact wording may vary but OLE applications have some way of indicating that you will return to Microsoft Access).

 If the data type is recognized by one of the registered OLE applications, the data (image, spreadsheet, PowerPoint slide) will appear in the OLE frame. If it isn't recognized an icon will appear instead. In either case, double-clicking on the data or icon will open the data in the parent OLE application.

How to Add Data to a Bound Object Frame

The procedure is very similar to that outlined for adding an unbound object frame to a form. The difference is how the process is initiated for a bound frame. This is the same procedure for adding data to a table or query field of the **OLE** data type.

Step 1.   Open the form in **Form** or **Form Layout View**.

Step 2.   Right click on the control bound to an **OLE** data type and select **Insert Object...** from the short cut menu.

Step 3.   Proceed with Step 3 from the previous procedure.

Image Control

This control displays images on a form or report. It differs from the **Bound** or **Unbound OLE Frames** in that the display is static - the user can't edit the image. Its advantage however is that it loads images much more quickly than either of the object frames.

The **Image Control** will not display images from a field of the **OLE** data type. If you intend to use this control as a bound control, one approach is to bind the **Image Control** to a text field that stores local or network path information about the location of an image.

A more common use of the **Image Control** is to load a static image, for example a group or corporate logo, that appears consistently on all forms and reports. In this mode the control is unbound to any data field.

How to Add an Unbound Image Control

This is the default for this control. When you place an **Image Control** on a form the **Insert Image** dialog box automatically appears. You can be in either **Form Layout** or **Form Design View** for this procedure.

Step 1.   From the **Controls** group select the **Image Control** and draw a rectangle on the form.

Step 2.   The **Insert Image** dialog box will appear. Navigate to the desired image file, select it, and choose **Open**.

Step 3.   The **Image Control** will appear with the selected image file displayed.

How to Add a Bound Image Control

The bound field should be of the **Text** data type. Field values should resolve to the local or network path to an image resource. Because the default control type for a field of the **Text** data type is a **Text Box**, you need to manually add the **Image Control** to your form and adjust its **Control Source** property. You can be in either **Form Layout** or **Form Design View** for this procedure.

Step 1.   From the **Controls** group select the **Image Control** and draw a rectangle on the form.

Step 2.   When the **Insert Image** dialog box appears, choose **Cancel**.

Step 3.   Open the **Property Sheet** for the **Image Control** and move to the **Data** tab.

Step 4.   Use the **Drop Down Box** associated with the **Control Source** property and select the desired field.

An **Image Control** by default only displays images with BMP, ICO, DIB, WMF or EMF formats. The control may display other formats depending upon additional graphics filters installed. It is normal to find that common file types such as GIF and JPG (or JPEG) are also handled. If in doubt, you may need to create a test condition and load several file formats to ensure that the **Image Control** behaves as expected.

If an **Image Control** is handed a file of an image type it does not support, the control will appear blank in **Form** and **Form Layout Views**.

Common Image Control Properties

Property	Description
Picture Type	Options are *Embedded*, *Linked*, or *Shared*. Embedded images are stored with the form. Link images use file location information, and Shared images come from the Access image gallery.
Picture	Displays the name of the image if it is Linked, Shared, or Embedded. If the image control is bound to a field containing file location information this field is blank.
Picture Tiling	If **Size Mode** is set to *Clip* and the image control is larger than the image, the image will repeat within the control. You can control alignment in this mode using the **Picture Alignment** property.
Size Mode	If **Size Mode** is set to *Clip* and the image control is larger than the image, the image will repeat within the control. You can control alignment in this mode using the **Picture Alignment** property.
Picture Alignment	Options are *Stretch*, *Clip*, and *Zoom*. *Clip* is the default and displays the actual size of the picture. If the control is smaller than the image not all of the image is displayed. *Stretch* sizes the picture to fill the control and may result in distortion if the height to width ratio of image and control are not the same. *Zoom* displays the entire picture, resizing as necessary to enable all of the image to be viewed with the control. Blank space may appear to the sides of the image.
Control Source	Creates a bound image control if the field stores the file path and name of a graphic file. If both this property and **Picture** are set, the value in the **Picture** property will only appear if the field value corresponding to the **Control Source** is blank, otherwise the **Control Source** takes priority over the **Picture** property.

Attachment Control

This bound control is relatively new to Microsoft Access (beginning with Access 2007). It manages data for fields of the new *Attachment* data type. Attachments differ from OLE data types in two regards: (1) the Attachment data type is not supported by other database management systems - it is exclusive to Microsoft Access, and (2) because it stores information about attachments as a reference rather than as an embedded object, using Attachments keeps database tables from becoming very large.

The Attachment control works the same as when working with a table in **Datasheet View**. You can manually add an Attachment control to a form or drag a field of the *Attachment* data type onto the form. You can work with this control in **Form Layout** and **Form Design View**.

Points on Attachment Controls

- This control acts to mediate the interaction between the data stored within a field of the **Attachment** data type and the various applications which manage the attached data.

- The attached data always reside *outside* the Microsoft Access application and in this sense act as *linked* OLE data. The difference being that **Attachments** always consume far less table storage space.

- The control can exhibit three icon views: Image/Icon, Icon, or PaperClip. In the first case if the attachment is a file extension that Windows understands, the user will see the appropriate associated icon. Example: An attached Microsoft Excel workbook will have the current Excel icon displayed in the attachment control.

- For fields that have two or more attachments, they appear one at a time within the control. The user must right-click on the control and choose **Manage Attachments** or **Forward/Backward** to move through attachments.

How to Manually Add an Attachment Control

The more straightforward way to add this control is to drag a field of the **Attachment** data type from the **Field List**.

Step 1.   From the **Controls** group, choose the **Attachment** control and draw a rectangle onto your form.

Step 2.   Open the **Property Sheet** for the control and adjust the appropriate settings. Use the following table as a guide.

Common Attachment Control Properties

Property	Description
Display As	Options are *Icon/Image*, *Icon*, or *PaperClip*. The default is *Image/Icon* - if the attachment is a graphic then an image is displayed, otherwise the icon of the associated application appears. With *Icon* all attachments display the icon associated with the registered application to manage that file type. Choosing *PaperClip* sets the display to a stock paper clip image regardless of the file type associated with the attachment.
Default Picture Type	Options are *Embedded*, *Linked*, or *Shared*. Embedded images are stored with the form. Link images use file location information, and Shared images come from the Access image gallery.
Default Picture	Displays a default image if the current record's field does not have any attachments. If attachments are present, the **Display As** property setting takes precedent.
Picture Tiling	If **Size Mode** is set to *Clip* and the image control is larger than the image, the image will repeat within the control. You can control alignment in this mode using the **Picture Alignment** property.
Picture Alignment	Options are *Stretch*, *Clip*, and *Zoom*. *Clip* is the default and displays the actual size of the picture. If the control is smaller than the image not all of the image is displayed. *Stretch* sizes the picture to fill the control and may result in distortion if the height to width ratio of image and control are not the same. *Zoom* displays the entire picture, resizing as necessary to enable all of the image to be viewed with the control. Blank space may appear to the sides of the image.
Picture Size Mode	If **Size Mode** is set to *Clip* and the image control is larger than the image, the image will repeat within the control. You can control alignment in this mode using the **Picture Alignment** property.
Control Source	Names the field the control is bound to. The field *must* be of the **Attachment** data type. If the current record's field is without attachments and a **Default Picture** has been selected, that value is displayed in the control, otherwise for records with **Attachments**, the value of the **Display As** property takes effect.

Chart Control

This control is actually an OLE object and represents an instance of Microsoft Graph, a shared component of the Microsoft Office Suite. When you add a **Chart** to a form the **Chart Wizard** begins regardless of the setting of **Use Control Wizards**.

The **Chart** is always a bound control but behaves differently depending upon the condition of the containing form. If the form is unbound the **Chart** will display static data. If the form is bound to data in a one-to-one or one-to-many relationship and the Chart Wizard can identify the linking fields, the **Chart** will update and display the related data as the form steps through its records.

Points on Chart Controls

- Charts can be complicated objects and this control is no exception. It may take time working with simple test data sets before you fully understand how the Microsoft Graph component works.

- If a chart is viewed in **Form** or **Form Design View** (but not **Form Layout View**), double clicking on the chart will open it in Microsoft Graph. In this mode you have many formatting options available to fine tune your chart. Clicking anywhere on the containing form will close Microsoft Graph and return you to the previous form view.

- When in Microsoft Graph a data sheet will display that contains the underlying data. This information may be edited although it will not be retained by a chart connected to a data source in Microsoft Access, nor will changing data from within Microsoft Graph modify the contents of an Access table.

- When Microsoft Graph is open you may use the **Help** menu to learn more about how Microsoft Graph works.

How to Add a Chart Control to an Unbound Form

This is the method to use if you need a chart that will display static data. You may want to size the form and the containing graph to be as large as possible. This should ensure that most of the chart elements created will be fully visible and that that point you can resize the **Chart** and/or Form as required.

Step 1.   Open an unbound form in **Form Design View**.

Step 2.   From the **Controls** group, select the **Chart** control and draw a rectangle on the form. The Chart Wizard will start and the first dialog box will appear similar to the following.

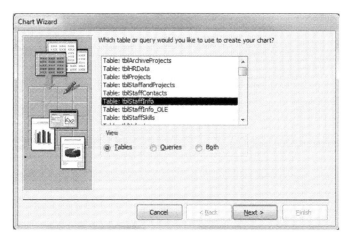

Step 3.   Select the data source for your chart. You may need to switch between **Tables** and **Queries** to locate your choice. Choose **Next** when ready. The second dialog box of the Chart Wizard will appear similar to the following:

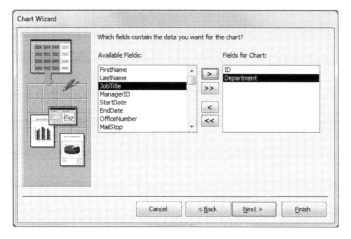

Step 4.   Choose the fields (generally you'll require a minimum of two) that will be used by the **Chart**. In this and the following examples the goal is to create a chart showing staffing levels by department. The *ID* field uniquely identifies each staff member and therefore can serve as a count. Once you have chosen the desired fields, choose **Next**. The next dialog box of the Chart Wizard will appear similar to the following.

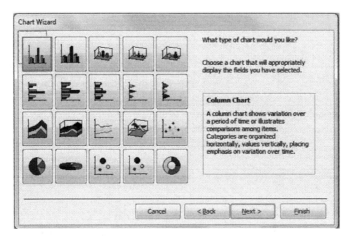

Step 5.   Select the type of chart to use. Note that not all chart types will work for the number of fields you selected in Step 4. Note also that you can change the chart type at any time once the Wizard has completed. Once your chart type has been selected, choose **Next**.

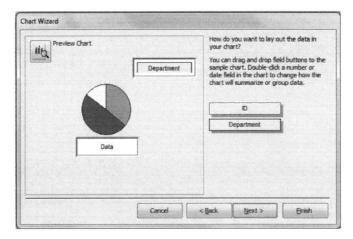

Step 6.   Drag the fields you selected in Step 4 to their appropriate location. Note that the location will depend upon the chart type you choose in the preceding step. Generally a drop box will be labeled **Data** and that is where the field that constitutes the values you wish to display will go (in this example, *ID* is the **Data** since we're interested in the number of staff per department). Another drop box will be labeled *ID* and, in the case of a simple pie chart, is where the *Department* field should be dragged. Once the fields have been placed to your satisfaction, choose **Next**.

Selecting **Preview Chart** will open a preview window where you can see sample data organized into the selected chart type. If the arrangement of data isn't correct, close the preview window and reorganize your fields in Step 6.

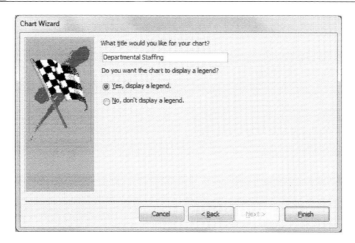

Step 7.   In the final dialog box, type a title for the Chart. You may also choose whether to display a legend. Choose **Finish**. A chart contained on a form will appear similar to the following.

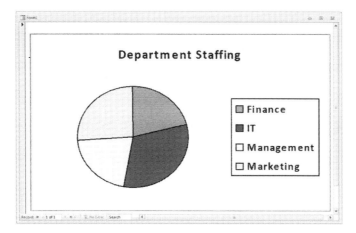

How to Add a Chart Control to a Bound Form

This is a useful way to display dynamic graphical data. The Chart Wizard is only capable of working with a single table or query, so you may need to create a query that contains fields from the various tables when working with a form and **Chart** that display related data.

In this procedure we will step though an example where the main form is linked to a table that displays data about *Projects* while the chart shows *Project Budget* data for the current *Project* broken down by *Department*.

There are several ways to construct such a bound **Chart**. In this example (working from the sample database *Staff and Projects*) we will create a form that is bound to the *tblProjects* table. A query containing budget and department information from the two other tables in this many-to-many relationship is illustrated below. We should note that creating a **Chart** to display data in a many-to-many relationship is, from the perspective of the underlying data, as complicated as it gets. Nonetheless, this is a good example to illustrate how to create such a bound object.

The **Relationship Window** from the *Staff and Projects* database for the three tables mentioned above appears as follows:

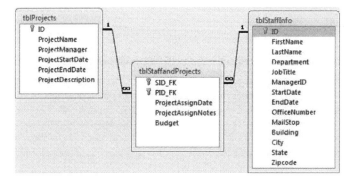

The query used to supply data for the **Chart** control appears as follows:

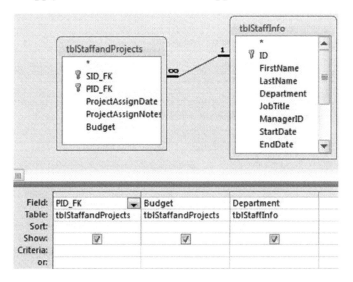

The parent form is bound to the *tblProjects* table and contains the Primary Key from that table (this will be used by the Chart Wizard to provide the linking information). The query includes the bridge table (linking *tblProjects* and *tblStaffInfo*). The bridge table contains the budget information since in this database each staff are provided a budget for each project they're assigned. The query also links to the *tblStaffInfo* table as that is where the *Department* information is stored.

Step 1.   Create a bound form containing the data from the *one* side of a *one-to-many* join, or the information of greatest interest if working with data in a *many-to-many* join. Add the desired fields but ensure that the Primary Key field is included on the form.

Step 2.   Create a query that contains the fields needed to supply data to the **Chart** control. Ensure that the Foreign Key field to the form's Primary Key is included in the query (it usually will not appear on the chart in any form but the Chart Wizard requires it to create the necessary **Child** and **Master Field** properties.

Step 3.   Size the form as necessary and in **Form Design View** add a **Chart** control.

Step 4.   Choose the data source for the **Chart** (in this example, the query illustrated above).

Step 5.   Choose the fields to be used by the **Chart**.

Step 6.   Choose the Chart Type.

Step 7.   Arrange the fields on the **Chart** to ensure that the field(s) which constitutes the **Data** and the field(s) which constitute the **Series** are correctly placed. Use the **Preview Chart** button as needed to ensure that the field placements are correct. Following that step (which maps to Step 6 from the procedure on working with an unbound **Chart**), the following dialog box - unique to working with a bound **Chart** will appear:

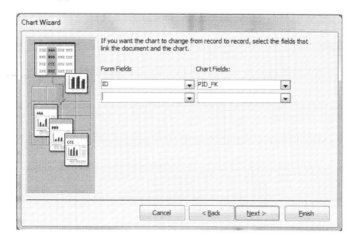

Step 8.   If the Wizard was unable to identify the linking Primary and Foreign Key fields (between parent form and chart data source), adjust the **Form Fields** and **Chart Fields** drop down boxes to manually establish this relationship. Choose **Next** when ready.

Step 9.   Provide a **Title** for your **Chart** and determine **Legend** visibility. Select **Finish** when ready. A bound **Chart** will appear on the form similar to the following:

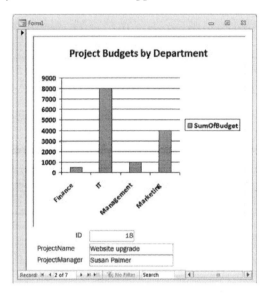

Moving to another project on the main form will force an update of the **Chart** as illustrated below.

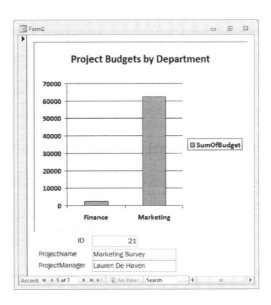

Common Chart Control Properties

Property	Description
Link Master Fields	Identifies the field or fields which constitute the Primary Key for the form.
Link Child Fields	Identifies the field or fields which make up the Foreign Key for the Chart's data source.
Row Source	The data source for the **Chart**. The wizard will generate a SQL query but inspection will reveal that the data source you chose is the data source for this SQL query.
Row Source Type	The default value is *Table/Query*. This property should not be altered as the other options, *Field List* and *Value List* are out of context with a **Chart**.

Hyperlink Control

The **Hyperlink** control really isn't a separate control type. When you place this object on a form the **Insert Hyperlink** dialog box opens and guides you through the process of creating a link to any number of targets. When the process is complete, the control is placed on the form as a **Label** with certain properties set.

This control is unbound (as are all Labels) and is not the control that is placed on a form when you drag a field of the **Hyperlink** data type from the **Field List**. In the latter case the control resolves to a **Text Box**.

Hyperlink controls are useful if you need the ability to open an object in Access, a Word document, Excel Workbook, or a PowerPoint slide presentation, or to jump to a web page or create an email message. Because this is an unbound control the hyperlink remains the same as you step through records if the control has been placed on a bound form. One good example for a **Hyperlink** control would be to create a link to your organization's home page that might appear on certain forms in the header or footer area.

The **Hyperlink** control can be made to emulate a bound control but this requires VBA programming. There is a book in this series, *Building VBA Apps Using Microsoft Access 2010* which addresses this topic.

Points on Hyperlink Controls

- A **Hyperlink** control really becomes a **Label** control, but with at a minimum the **Hyperlink** property of the **Label** set.

- **Hyperlinks** can link to the following document types: web pages (and if known, jump to a specific *bookmark* on that page), Word documents (and if known, jump to a specific *bookmark* in the document), Excel workbooks (with a jump to a specific named *range* if desired), a PowerPoint presentation (with a jump to a specific *slide*, if desired), any other object within the current Access database. The **Hyperlink** can also create an email message with the *Recipient Address* and *Subject* lines pre-entered.

How to Use the Hyperlink Control

You can be in **Form Layout** or **Form Design View** when creating this control.

Step 1.   From the **Controls** group, select the **Hyperlink** control. Draw a rectangle (if in **Form Layout** view) or hover the mouse over the form (in **Form Design** view). The **Insert Hyperlink** dialog box will appear as illustrated below.

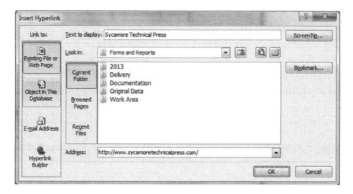

Step 2.   Select the desired **Link to** category, and if required, choose a subcategory. The following table describes the options for this dialog box.

Option	Description
Existing File or Web Page	To link an existing file, use the **Current Folder** button or the **Look in**, **Up one Folder**, or **Browse for File** controls to locate the target file. The **Recent Files** control will display recent Microsoft Office documents you have worked with.
	To select a Web page, either manually enter an address in the **Address** text area or select **Browse the Web** control.
Object in This Database	Displays a hierarchal list of all objects in the current database. You can jump (open) any Table, Query, Form, Report, Macro or Module.
E-mail Address	Creates a blank email form where you complete the recipient address and a subject line (if desired).
Hyperlink Builder	Used to create hyperlinks to web pages that accept *parameters* or where you wish to drill down to a specific directory.

Step 3.   Select the target object (for **Object in This Database**) or file (for files located on your computer or local area network, or type a web or email address. Choose **OK** when done.

As previously mentioned, the **Hyperlink** control is in actuality just a **Label** with some properties set for you. The following table highlights those properties.

Common Hyperlink (Label) Properties

Property	Description
Caption	Controls the text used to display the hyperlink address. If you do not specify a caption Access uses the value of the **Hyperlink** property.
Fore Color	The default is *Hyperlink Color,* which appears as blue text. If you choose another color scheme consider keeping the **Font Underline** property set to *Yes* to provide a visual clue to users that this is a hyperlink.
Font Underline	The default is *Yes* so hyperlinks display as underlined text.
Hyperlink Address	Specifies the target for the hyperlink. This resolves to an HTTP, MailTo, File, or Access object reference. If you specified *Paths* and/or *Parameters* they are included in this property.
Hyperlink SubAddress	If the hyperlink is configured to jump to a specific web or Word document bookmark, to a named range in an Excel workbook, or to a slide in a PowerPoint slideshow, that target is specified here.
Hyperlink Target	Controls where in a browser the hyperlink page appears. This property maps to the HTML anchor element *Target* attribute.

Web Browser Control

This control places an instance of Microsoft Internet Explorer on a form. When bound, the control displays web pages accessed through its **Control Source** property. If unbound the control simply displays the same page regardless of what record the form is on, although if the page contains navigation links the user can browse those links.

There is no navigation bar or other elements of the standard user interface (no menus, bookmarks, history, etc.), although right-clicking on the control in **Form View** will display a few browser-related functions such as **Back** and **Forward** (when in the correct context). As a result, this control should not be used to provide browsing functionality to your form users. It is a very useful control for displaying web (or intranet) data that resolves on a record-by-record basis. After a discussion of how to use the control (it is one of the controls for which the **Control Wizard** is evoked), we'll step through an example using Google Maps to map street addresses using the **Browser** control.

Points on the Web Browser Control

- The control uses an instance of the version of Microsoft Explorer installed on the computer running your application. You cannot substitute another browser such as Mozilla Firefox.

- There are no zoom levels or other features of the standard Microsoft Internet Explorer interface available. Scroll bars will appear when the displayed content is larger than the **Web Browser** control, but you may need to test this control and its size on your form before releasing it for use.

- The control displays a web page as the URL is stored in a bound field. There isn't an easy way for the end user to navigate to a new web page so this control is best used to display web data on a record-by-record basis. Example, based on the current record on the form, to display a map based on an address or to display product information from a corporate website.

- If you are using a website that publishes information about passing parameters, it's easier to use the **Control Wizard** to step through the process of generating a syntactically correct URL. You may need to experiment with an actual web browser before getting your application to perform as expected.

How to Use the Browser Control Wizard

If you intend to configure this as a bound control, the field containing the URL information must be present on the form (it can be hidden if desired). You can be in **Form Layout** or **Form Design** view to work with this control.

Step 1.   Ensure that the **Use Control Wizards** option is enabled, then select the **Web Browser** control and drag a rectangle on your form. The **Insert Hyperlink** dialog box should appear as follows:

Step 2.   If you wish to use the control unbound, enter a valid web address in the **Address** text area, and choose **OK**. This completes this procedure. If you wish to use the control bound to a field on the form, select the **Builder (…)** associated with the **Base URL** text box. The **Expression Builder** will appear similar to the following:

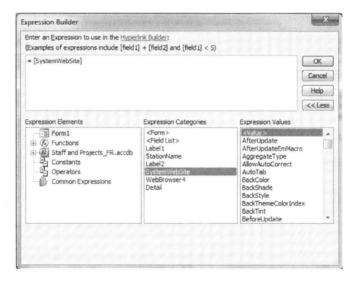

Step 3.   Select the current form from the **Expression Elements** area, then choose the desired field to bind from the **Expression Categories**. Finally, double-click on the **<Value>** property in the **Expression Values** list. The name of the field

should appear following an equal sign in the upper display area. Choose **OK** when done.

Step 4.   Choose **OK** to complete the **Control Wizard**.

 If you know the field name you can enter it directly in the **Base URL** text box in Step 2.

 When the form is opened in **Form** or **Form Layout View** the **Web Browser** will display the URL in its **Control Source** property. If bound to a field containing URL values, the **Web Browser** will change content as you step through records on the form.

Case Study: Using the Web Browser Control to Display Google Map Data

This is a straightforward use of the **Web Browser** control. You need to understand how Google Maps requires address data in order to proceed. Other mapping services will approach address data differently. When in doubt, research the requirements to use a particular web service by passing *parameters* along in the URL.

In the case of Google Maps, these are the salient points:

- The **Base URL** is http://google.com
- The **Path** is *map*
- The **Parameter** is *q=[URL-Ready Address]*

As an example, to get Google Maps to display a map of Washington DC, centered on the White House, you would enter the following text in a web browser:

http://google.com/maps?q=1600+Pensylvania+Avenue+Washington+DC+20500

A *URL-Ready Address* does not contain spaces. Each space has been replaced by a plus sign (+). This isn't a problem if you are building an URL-ready address and none of your fields contain spaces - but generally they do. The address *1600 Pennsylvania Avenue* contains two spaces. So if you have a table with the following fields: *[Address]*, *[City]*, *[State]*, and *[PostalCode]* one way to convert your address fields into a URL-Ready field would be to create a query based on your address table. Create a new field named *URLReadyAddress* and enter the following expression:

URLReadyAddress: Replace([Address] & "+" & [City] & "+" & [State] & "+" & [ZipCode]," ","+")

The expression uses the **Replace()** function which accepts three required arguments: The string to work on (in this case it is a string that also contains instructions for concentration: [Address] & "+" & [City] & "+" & [State] & "+" & [PostalCode] where the individual field values are concatenated with a plus sign between each field value. The second argument of the **Replace()** function is the string value to replace. That's denoted by the " " (double-quote space double-quote) - in other words we want **Replace()** to locate spaces within any of our address fields and replace them. The final argument, "+", is the character to replace spaces with.

If you create a query with such a function and include any other fields you would like on your form, you're ready to create a map-enabled form.

Step 1.   Open a blank form and adjust its **Record Source** property so the form is bound to the query you created that contains URL-ready field values.

Step 2.   Ensure that **Use Control Wizards** is enabled and draw a **Web Browser** control on your form. The **Insert Hyperlink** dialog box will appear as illustrated in Step 2 of the previous procedure.

Step 3.   In the **Base URL** text area, type *http://google.com*

Step 4.   In the **Paths** text area, type *maps*

Step 5.   In the **Parameters** area in the **Name** column, type *q*

Step 6.   Move to the **Value** column and either type *=[Field Name]* where field name is the name of the field in your query that contains the **Replace()** function, or use the **Builder(...)** to locate the field on the current form. When done the **Insert Hyperlink** dialog box should look similar to the following.

Step 7.   Choose **OK** to complete the Wizard. When you open your form in **Form** or **Form Layout** view and step between records containing valid street addresses, the **Web Browser** will display a Google Map with the street address noted.

An example, using the street address of the *Eastern Market* metro station in Washington, DC is presented below:

Page Break Control

Although this control is available to both forms and reports, its use is more meaningful when applied to a report. The Page Break control is discussed beginning on page 220.

Chapter 7 | Calculated Controls

A *Calculated Control* is an unbound control that uses an expression as its *Row Source* property. Calculated controls may be used for a variety of purposes, including:

- Display system information such as today's date or the current report page number.

- Refer to bound controls on the current form or report, on subforms or subreports contained by the current form or report, or on other open forms or reports.

- Show the results of arithmetic functions such as **Sum** or **Avg**. The scope or how much data the control works with, is dependent upon where it is located on the form or report. Controls on the Detail section of a form or a report only "see" one record at a time. Controls on Header or Footer sections "see" all the records in the recordset. This rule applies to subforms and subreports as well.

- Display the results of Domain Aggregate Functions to summarize information across an entire recordset.

Points on Calculated Controls

- A calculated control can present the results of a simple function, total values between other fields, combine field values and functions, and/or refer to controls on other sections of a form or report, or refer to controls on other, open forms or reports.

- The most common calculated controls include the **Text Box, Option Button, Check Box and Toggle Button**. The last three controls are used to display the results of expressions which resolve to either **True** or **False.**

- **Text Box** controls may display either text, date/time or numeric data.

- The **Label** control cannot be used as a calculated control because it lacks the row source property.

- The expression for a calculated control may be entered in the **Row Source** property of the control's **Property List,** or in the case of **Text Box** controls, the expression may be entered directly in the control using **Edit Mode**.

- For controls that employ summary functions such as **Count()** or **Sum()**, the scope of the function will change depending upon where on a form or report the calculated control is located. Placed in the **Detail** section, the control may only "*see*" one record at a time. When placed on a form **Header** or **Footer**, or on reports, in any of the **Group Header** or **Group Footer** areas the scope broadens. For forms the control can count or sum across all bound records. For reports, depending upon what type of section the control is in, it has access to grouped records or the entire recordset.

- When creating *Expressions* it is a good idea to enclose table and field names in square brackets *[ ]*. Often the **Expression Builder** will do this automatically. Square brackets are *required* in an expression if the table or field name contains blank spaces. When you have two fields with the same name from two or more tables it is also required that you use the syntax [table name].[field name] Example: [tblStaffInfo].[FirstName] and [tblHRData].[FirstName]

- A calculated control on a form *may not* be edited when the form is open in either **Form Layout** or **Form View**.

How to Manually Create a Calculated Control

Step 1.   Open the desired form in **Form Design View** and select the desired control, or add one of the following controls: **Text Box**, **Check Box**, **Option Button**, or **Toggle Button** to the form.

Step 2.   If working with a **Text Box**, you can enter the expression directly into the text area. Otherwise, open the **Property Sheet** for the control and move to the **Data** tab, then enter the **Control Source** text area.

Step 3.   Type the desired expression. Expressions *always* begin with an equals sign.

Step 4.   To test your expression open the form in **Form Layout** or **Form View**.

Examples of Expressions in a Text Box Control

Example	Description
=Date()	Displays the system date, as formatted in the **International System Settings** for the computer.
="Main Menu"	The text box will display the phrase *Main Menu*.
="Today is " & date()	Displays the text *Today is* followed by the system date. Example: **Today is 03/20/2014**
=[Salary] + [TotalBenefits]	Totals the contents of the *Salary* and *TotalBenefits* fields.
="The hotel cost is " & [Hotel] & " dollars"	Displays the text *The hotel cost is* followed by the value of the *Hotel* field. Example: **The hotel cost is 550 dollars**
=Sum([Budget])	Sums the contents of all *Budget* fields on the form. If this control is located in a form **Header** or **Footer** section, it sums all the *Budget* fields in the form's recordset.
=Forms![frmProjects]![txtProjectName]	Displays the contents of the control named *txtProjectName* located on a form named *frmProjects*. This type of expression is used to refer to the value of a control on *another* form. The *frmProjects* form must be open for the expression to be resolved correctly.
=Forms![frmProjects]![StaffingSubform]![txtSumofBudget]	Displays the contents of a control named *txtSumofBudget* located on the *StaffingSubform* subform on the form *frmProjects*. In this example it should be noted that the expression clearly follows a hierarchy between form, subform and then control. This type of *object path* is required of Access when referring to a child of a child of a parent.

Examples of Expressions for a Yes/No Control

Example	Description
=TRUE	Control will always indicate the Yes/True/On state.
=IIf(Hour(Now())<12,True,False)	Displays the Yes/True/On state if the time is before noon, otherwise displays the No/False/Off state.
=Forms![frmPrint]![chkPrintPreview]	Will display the state of a checkbox named *chkPrintPreview* located on a form named *frmPrint*.

Working with the Expression Builder

For complex expressions, you may wish to use the **Expression Builder**. The **Expression Builder** is a tool that gives you access to all of the object names in the current database as well as references to their property values. All of the built-in functions, including the **Domain Aggregate Functions,** are available, as well as any custom functions that have been created in a VBA module.

How to Create a Calculated Expression Using the Expression Builder

Step 1.   Activate the desired control and open the **Property Sheet**.

Step 2.   In the **Field Properties** area, select the **Data** tab.

Step 3.   Select the **Builder (…)** associated with the **Control Source** property. The **Expression Builder** will appear similar to the following:

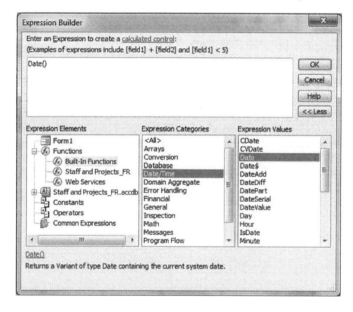

Components of the Expression Builder

Component	Description
Expression Box	Displays the expression as it is being built. You can directly enter text in this area or select **Operators** or items from the **Function List**.
Expression Elements	A list of the major categories of functions and objects available. All objects in the current database (including Forms and Reports and their associated controls) are available.
Expression Categories	Displays major categories associated with the currently selected item in the **Expression Element** list. If you choose *Built-In Functions* from the **Expression Elements**, this control will list categories of functions. If you choose an open form or report, this element will display all controls on that form or report.
Expression Values	Lists all functions contained within the category selected in the **Categories** list. Double-clicking an item will insert it into the **Expression Box**. For functions, this area will list all functions for the category selected in the **Expression Categories** area. For a control this area will list all properties and events for that control.
Help Area	If an Expression Value is selected, a brief description of the function as well as its argument list (if applicable) appears in the lower portion of the dialog box. The function name is a hyperlink and clicking on it opens on-line help for that function.

Step 4. Select a major category from the **Expression Elements** list. If the target folder displays a plus (+) you must double-click on it to display subfolders.

Step 5. From the **Categories** list select a category.

Step 6. From the **Function List** select a function. Double-click on the function to insert it into the **Expression Box** or use the **Paste** button.

Step 7. If arguments are required of the function, add them in the appropriate location within the function's *argument list*.

Step 8. Continue with Steps 4 through 7 as required to continue building your expression.

Step 9. Complete your expression and return to the **Query Design View** by choosing **OK**.

 For functions with 2 or more arguments, it's a good idea to review the on-line help topic. Some arguments are required, others are optional, and each may have a specific data type. All of these conditions are outlined in the help topic.

Function Categories

Category	Description
Arrays	Functions for determining array size.
Conversion	Functions that convert between data types.
Database	Tasks for creating database objects and obtaining system information.
Date/Time	General functions for manipulating date/time information.
Domain Aggregate	Tasks for providing statistical information about records in a recordset.
Error Handling	General error handling functions.
Financial	Functions for calculating a variety of financial tasks. These functions are a subset of those found in Microsoft Excel.
General	Generalized functions that do not easily fit into any of the other categories.
Inspection	Tasks to determine the state of a field value (such as whether it is empty or null).
Math	Standard mathematical functions.
Messages	Functions that will display input or message boxes.
Program Flow	Functions that can make decisions and control the overall flow of the expression.
SQL Aggregate	Similar to the **Domain Aggregate** functions, but part of the SQL language (the **Domain Aggregate** functions are not SQL-standard).
Text	General tasks for manipulating text data.

Common System Functions

Function	Description
Date()	Inserts the system date.
Time()	Inserts the system time.
Now()	Inserts a combination of the system date and time.
Page	Inserts the current page (only available to forms or reports when viewed in **Print Preview** or when printed).
Pages	Inserts the total number of pages (only available to forms or reports when viewed in **Print Preview** or when printed).

Common Arithmetic Operators and Functions

Operator or Function	Example	Description
+	=[Salary]+[Benefits]	Adds numeric values.
&	="Today is " & Date()	Concatenates values (no addition operation is applied).
-	=[TotalBudget] - [Materials]	Subtracts numeric values.
/	=[TotalBudget]/[Materials]	Divides numeric values.
Avg()	=Avg([TotalBudget])	Calculates the average value.
Count()	=Count([ProjectID])	Returns the number of values counted.
Max()	=Max([Budget])	Returns the highest value encountered.
Min()	=Min([Budget])	Returns the lowest value encountered.
Sum()	=Sum([Budget])	Calculates the sum of all values.

 You may need to edit the expression as it is being built. Some functions and operators will insert the text «Expr» or arguments within double angle brackets. This indicates a placeholder where you should enter expression text.

Calculated Controls on Forms

When you create a calculated control that refers to the value of a field (in other words a bound control), the *scope* of the calculated control is related to its location on the form. This interplay between control scope, or what the control *"sees"* is noticeable on forms that present data in *Continuous Form* view and also for forms that contain subforms, again especially if the subform displays multiple records. For example:

- A calculated control located in the Detail section only "sees" the current record. Use this location when you need expressions that work with fields in the current record.

- Placing a calculated control in the Header or Footer of a form or subform gains access to all records from the form or subform's recordset. This is the location to use when summarizing records.

- A calculated control on a form that refers to a control on a subform uses a formal expression that names the Forms collection, the current form, the name of the subform control and finally the name of the target control. An exclamation point (!)(also called the Bang operator) separates each object name. Example: To refer to the txtTotalProjectBudget control on the sbfProjectStaffing subform on the frmProjects form, the expression would appear as: =[Forms]![frmProjects]![sbfProjectStaffing]![txtTotalProjectBudget].

- A control on a subform can refer to a control on the containing (or parent) form using the Parent keyword. For a control on a subform to refer to a control named LastName on the parent form, the expression would appear as: =Parent![LastName].

- For controls that refer to the value of another control on another open form, a similar approach to the previous one is used. You name the Forms collection, then name the target form and finally name the target control on that form. Example: To refer to the txtDepartment control on a form named frmStaffInformation, the expression would appear as: =[Forms]![frmStaffInformation]![txtDepartment].

Example of Calculated Controls on a Form and Subform

Consider a form and subform that display project information (master form) and staffing information, including the budget assigned to each staff member (subform). The form in **Form View** would appear as:

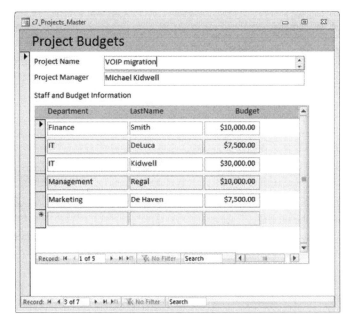

The same form opened in **Form Design View** would appear as:

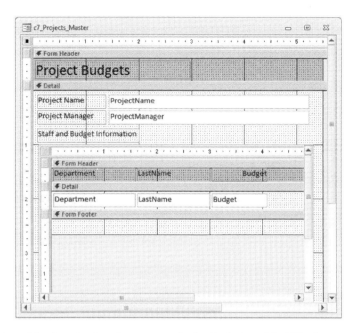

A snapshot of the tables involved as they appear in the **Relationship Window** appears below.

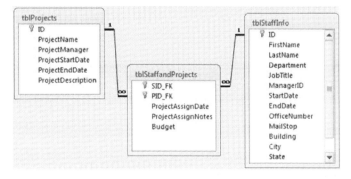

There are several points to make about these forms:

- The relationship is basically a one-to-many with Projects (master form) residing on the *one* side of the join and staffing and budget information (subform) modeled on the *many* side. Each project can have many staff assigned to it. In this database, each staff member is also given an individual budget for that project.

- The budget information appears only in the **Detail** section of the subform. This form's **Default View** property has been set to *Continuous Forms* so all of the records on the *many* side of the join can be viewed together.

- If we place a **Text Box** control (named *txtBudgetAdjustment*) in the subform **Detail** area, just to the right of the existing *Budget* bound control and set the **Control Source** property to =*[Budget] * 1.1* when the form is viewed each calculated control will correctly increase the individual budget amounts by 10%. The illustration only focuses in on the subform:

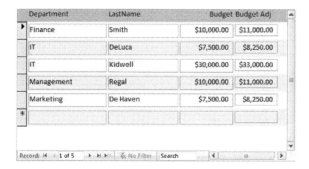

To create calculated controls that total the budget and the new budget adjustment for each project:

- Place a **Text Box** control (named *txtSumofBudget*) in the subform's **Footer** area. The **Control Source** property should appear as: =*SUM([Budget])* This control will sum the values of the *Budget* fields in the **Detail** area of the subform.

- Place a second **Text Box** control alongside the first control (named *txtSumofAdjBudget*). It's **Control Source** property should appear as =*SUM([Budget]*1.1)*.

To create a control on the **subform** that refers to a control on the main (master) form:

- Place a **Text box** control in the **Footer** of the subform. For the **Control Source** property enter the expression: =*"TOTAL FOR " & Parent![ProjectName]*

The three new calculated controls, all located in the **Footer** for the **Subform** would appear as:

To refer to a control (in this case we will refer to the value of the *txtSumofBudget* control) on the **Subform** (named *sbfProjectStaffing*) from the master form (named *frmProjects*):

- Place a **Text Box** control on the main form. For the **Control Source** property enter the expression: =*Forms![frmProjects]![sbfProjectStaffing]![txtSumofBudget]*

Lastly, if you need to refer to the total of all projects you need to rely on a *Domain Aggregate Function*. The reason being that in this database the *Budget* information resides on a table separate from the *Projects*. In the current form configuration it isn't possible to *"see"* all the budget data at once since the **subform** only displays those data for the current project. A domain aggregate function, DSUM() can handle this task. This function takes the form:

DSUM([field name], [table name], [optional *Where* condition])

To sum all *Budget* field values from the *tblStaffandProjects* table (and without any conditional filtering) the expression becomes =DSUM([Budget], [tblStaffandProjects]). This expression becomes a bit more useful in the present example if we can relate the current project total budget as a percentage of *all* project budgets. The last control placed on the main form then is a **Text Box** with a **Control Source** property set to:

=([txtProjectBudget]/DSum("[Budget]","[tblStaffandProjects]"))

These controls, taken together would appear as follows on the form originally illustrated on page 166 (the calculated controls have had their **Border Width** property set to *3 pt* for easy recognition:

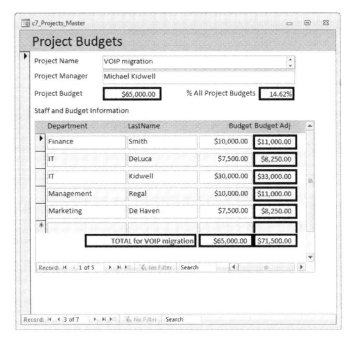

A summary of the controls, their location, and their **Control Source** settings appears in the following table.

Control	Control Source Expression
Calculated control in *Detail* section of subform (named txtBudgetAdjustment).	=[Budget] * 1.1
Calculated control in *Footer* section of subform (named txtSumofBudget).	=SUM([Budget])
Calculated control in *Footer* section of subform (named txtSumofBudgetAdjustment).	=SUM([Budget] * 1.1)
Control on subform referencing controls on the master form	="TOTAL for " & Parent![ProjectName] *(or)* =Forms![frmProjects]![ProjectName]
Control on master form referencing the value of a control on the subform (here txtSumofBudget). This control is named txtProjectBudget.	=Forms![frmProjects]![sbfProjectStaffing]![txtSumofBudget]
Control Using Domain Aggregate Function for Grand Total.	=([txtProjectBudget]/DSum("[Budget]","[tblStaffandProjects]"))

The 3rd referenced control uses the expression =SUM([Budget] * 1/1) rather than =SUM([txtBudgetAdjustment]) because Access cannot keep track of the value of the *txtBudgetAdjustment* control because it isn't a bound field and it appears numerous times since the subform is displaying *Continuous Forms*. Referring to the value of a calculated control works on the last line in the previous table since those controls are on the main form which is displaying one record at a time.

Domain Aggregate functions such as DSUM() are explained in more detail in the book *Building Queries Using Microsoft Access 2010*, which is part of this series.

Chapter 8 | Special Form Topics

This chapter focuses on two classes of special forms: the first are typically unbound and serve as switchboards, menus, and dialog boxes. They generally lack navigation controls and other features which by default appear on bound forms. The second class are bound and are bound to tables related in a many-to-many relationship. The **Form Wizard** can easily create forms that display many-to-many relationships but you'll discover that the subform may contain fields that are not editable. Adding new records to the subform is also typically a problem. We'll discuss why these issues arise and explore methods to circumvent them so your end users can fully edit data on both sides of a many-to-many relationship using a form.

Microsoft formerly provided a Switchboard Wizard to guide you through the process of creating a menu form. They now offer the **Navigation Form** as a tool for creating switchboards. While this control is useful, it cannot call another switchboard, thus making nested menu systems unavailable. Creating an unbound form manually is a good way to learn about this useful class of forms.

Overview of Unbound Forms

Unbound forms serve generalized user interface, maintenance, and administrative functions in a database. They contain controls that support specific tasks for the form. If it is necessary that a control display some data from the database, many developers rely on calculated controls that use **Domain Aggregate Functions** rather than by binding the form to a record source. Unbound forms, as suppliers of generalized database tasks, are typically configured as *dialog boxes*.

Points on Unbound Forms (Dialog Boxes)

- Because the form is unbound, record selectors, record navigators, and other controls associated with moving through a recordset should be removed.

- The form is generally not sizable (e.g. , the user cannot change the shape of the form).

- If the form is *modal*, it must be closed before any other form in the database can receive the focus.

- A pop-up form floats over all other objects in the database. If the form blocks important views ensure that there is a clear way to close it.

- If the dialog box is serving as a *Display Form* it automatically opens when the database is opened. Display Forms serve as great main menu forms.

Switchboard Forms

Switchboard forms are used to open other forms, reports, tables, or queries in the database. They present the overall database and its associated tasks as a series of forms giving the user choices. From the user's perspective, there is no need to understand how to use the **Navigation Pane** or manage individual database objects.

Many developers will use the **Command Button Wizard** to quickly create the individual command buttons for a switchboard form. Once the buttons have been created, specific form properties are adjusted to create a dialog box form. Lastly, if the form is intended to open when the database is opened, specific database properties are also set.

How to Create a Switchboard Form

This form type should be created only after the majority of basic data entry forms and database reports have been created.

Step 1.   Create a new form by choosing **Blank Form** from the **Forms** group on the **Create** tab. When the form appears, close the **Field List** and switch to **Form Design View**.

Step 2.   Enable **Use Control Wizards** and begin by adding the first **Command Button** to the form. In the wizard, set the **Command Button** to open the desired form, report, table or query. Refer to the procedure starting on page 120.

Step 3.   Repeat adding **Command Buttons** for each desired menu option.

Step 4.   If desired, add **Label** controls to create form titles or instructive text. Refer to page 85 for details.

Step 5.   If desired, add **Line** and/or **Rectangle** controls to group related **Command Buttons** or form regions. See the procedures starting on page 123 for details.

Step 6.   Adjust form properties to create a dialog box. Refer to page 36 for procedures on adjusting form properties, and to the following table for important properties.

Step 7.   Save your form.

 Recall from Chapter 6 that using the ampersand (&) as part of a command button's **caption** property creates an *accelerator key*. These are useful user interface elements and are generally expected in Windows applications.

Important Form Properties to Create a Dialog Box

Property	Property Setting/Description
Default View	*Single Form.*
Views Allowed	*Form.*
Scroll Bars	*Neither.* Scroll bars are not typically associated with switchboard forms. Consider breaking the form into smaller, related forms if required.
Record Selectors	*No.* Unbound forms should not display record selectors.
Navigation Buttons	*No* (Same as above).
Dividing Lines	*No.*
Auto Center	Yes. Generally switchboard forms appear in the center of the screen when opened.
Border Style	*Dialog* if you do not want users resizing, maximizing or minimizing the form. *Thin* if you do not want users to resize the form. They can maximize or minimize it however.
Control Box	*Yes* if you want to give users the option to close or move the form using the **Control Box Menu**), *No* if you want to remove the menu.
Min Max Buttons	*Yes* if you want to give users the option to maximize or minimize the form, No if you wish to remove this ability. Note that setting the **Border Style** to Dialog sets this property to *No.*
Close Button	*Yes* if you want to have a standard **Close** button on the form window), or *No* if you wish this feature removed. Important Note: Do Not remove the **Close** button and the **Control Box** without giving users another way to close the form!
Pop Up	*Yes* if the form should float above all other open database objects or *No* if the form can permit other objects to float over it. Note: if you intend that the form remain open while the database is being used, set this property to *No.*
Modal	*Yes* if the form must be closed before any other database object can be manipulated or *No* if the user can freely switch between database objects. Generally unless the form demands the user's attention, set this property to *No.*

How to Specify Startup Options

Startup options control how your database appears and behaves when it is opened in Microsoft Access. One of the options is to specify a **Display Form**, which is one of your forms that will automatically appear when the database is opened. This is a good property for a form that serves as a main or starting menu.

Step 1.   Choose the **File** tab, then select **Options**.

Step 2.   On the **Access Options** dialog box, in the left-hand navigation pane, select **Current Database**. Adjust the properties using the following table as a guide.

Option	Description
Application Title	Sets the text that will appear in the Access **Title Bar**.
Application Icon	Specifies an icon file that will serve as the icon for the database. This icon will appear in the Access **Title Bar.**
Use as Form and Report Icon	If you choose an **Application Icon**, checking this box places the icon on the title bars for all forms and reports.
Menu Bar	Controls whether the standard (default) or a custom menu bar is used at startup.
Display Form	Indicates the form to automatically open at database startup.
Display Status Bar	Specifies whether the **Status Bar** is visible.
Document Window Options	The choices are *Overlapping Windows* or *Tabbed Documents* (default). The first choice presents all database objects in individual windows which may be freely moved. The latter option opens all objects within a tab control-like interface.
Use Navigation Keys	Enables the use of the *F11* key sequence to open the **Navigation Pane**.
Use Windows-themed controls on Forms	If enabled, Form controls inherit Microsoft Office Themes.
Enable Layout View	Disable if you do not wish to grant your end users the ability to work in **Form Layout View**.
Display Navigation Pane	If unchecked, the **Navigation Pane** will not appear when the database is opened. If you disable **Use Navigation Keys** as well, the **Navigation Pane** is not available.

Step 3.   Adjust database **Startup** options, if desired.

Step 4.   Choose **OK.**

Warning: It is possible to render the Access user interface unworkable by selecting some combinations of **Startup** options. If you need to open a database file and bypass the **Startup** options, hold down the *Shift* key while opening the database file.

Data Entry Forms and Many-to-Many Joins

Modeling a *many-to-many* relationship using forms is pretty straightforward - as long as you are mainly interested in either viewing data or conducting data entry or editing in the tables that constitute either of the *many* sides of the relationship. In fact, using the **Form Wizard** is an easy way to create a form and subform that can display data from this relationship type.

An issue arises if you wish to enter new data in the intermediary, or *bridge table*. Usually the Form Wizard doesn't include the foreign key fields in that table and if it does, they are generally ID fields - recall that in a bridge table at a minimum you must include foreign key fields that map to each of the primary key fields in the tables modeling the *many* side of the relationship. To illustrate this issue consider the following many-to-many join from a staff and projects database:

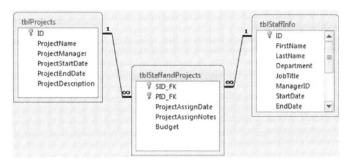

In the illustrated relationship, *tblProjects* and *tblStaffInfo* are joined in a many-to-many relationship via the bridge table *tblStaffandProjects*. This bridge table stores the real-world facts that each staff member may be on zero to many projects and each project may have zero to many staff. For each staffing event (assignment of a staff member to a particular project), the project ID from the *tblProjects* table (the field is *PID_FK*) and the staff ID from the *tblStaffInfo* tables are stored as a single record in the *tblStaffandProjects* bridge table.

To add staff to project using a form based on projects, you'd need to know the staff *ID* value in order to complete the record correctly in the *tblStaffand Projects* table. You don't need to know the project ID since the form and subform are managing that side of the many-to-many relationship. This is the problem in creating forms that support full data entry for many-to-many relationships.

The solution is to add a **Combo** or **List Box control** to the subform. **Combo** and **List Boxes** are unique in that they can display data from one source yet bind one of the displayed (or hidden) fields to another record source. Set its properties so the display values are derived from the *primary key* field of the *many* table (**Row Source** property), but the value is stored (**Control Source** property) in the *foreign key* field of the *bridge table* (these properties are discussed beginning on page 86). This would allow you to display staff first and last names in the **Combo** or **List Box** control, yet store the staff *ID* value in the *SID_FK* (which is the foreign key field for staff ID) in the bridge table. The following illustration shows this in action. The combo box pulls Staff *ID*, *FirstName*, and *LastName* values from the *tblStaffInfo* table. When you make a selection the Staff *ID* value is placed in the *SID_FK* field in the *tblStaffand Projects* bridge table.

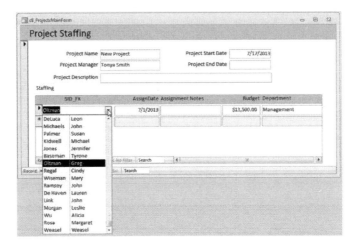

Example: Creating a Data Entry Form Based on a Many-to-Many Join

We will step through this example using the tables and fields discussed above. The key point will be altering the control bound to the foreign key field to ensure that, in this case, staff *ID* is stored in the bridge table.

The **Form Wizard** will be used to create the initial form and subform, then the **Combo Box Wizard** will be used to modify the design of the subform.

Step 1. Create a form using the **Form Wizard**. Add the desired fields from the table of primary interest in the *many-to-many* join. In this case fields from the *tblProjects* table are of primary interest since this is a form designed to manage project staffing.

Step 2. While adding fields, move to the bridge table and at a minimum, add the foreign key field that corresponds to the primary key field from the *other* table. In the example we've been working with, this is the field *SID_FK*. This bridge table also houses useful information about each project:staff assignment - namely the budget assigned to each staff for each project as well as the date of the project assignment and a field to store notes about the assignment.

Step 3. If desired, add fields from the *other* table which may be useful. The following table highlights the fields and their ultimate location on the form/subform pair.

Location	Table	Field
Form	tblProjects	**ProjectName**
	tblProjects	ProjectManager
	tblProjects	ProjectStartDate, ProjectEndDate
	tblProjects	ProjectDescription
Subform	tblStaffandProjects	SID_FK (foreign key to Staff *ID*)
	tblStaffandProjects	ProjectAssignDate
	tblStaffandProjects	ProjectAssignNotes
	tblStaffandProjects	Budget
	tblStaffInfo	Department

The other foreign key field required of the bridge table, *FK_PID*, which maps to the project *ID* field in the *tblProjects* table isn't required. Because these relationships were established in the **Relationships Window**, the Wizard knows to include this primary/foreign key pair in the **Link Master Fields** and **Link Child Fields** properties of the **Subform** control.

Step 4.   Continue stepping through the Wizard to build the initial form and subform. When completed (and following a few design changes to size and move controls around), the form and subform will appear similar to the following. Note the staff *ID* data in the *SID_FK* field.

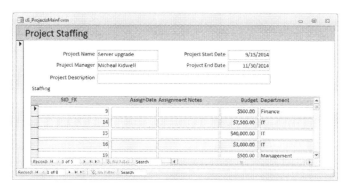

Step 5.   Switch to **Form Design View** and, if desired open the **Subform** in another window (otherwise, select the subform control). Select the **Text Box** bound to bridge table foreign key (here it's the *SID_FK* field) and delete it.

Step 6.   Ensure that **Use Control Wizards** is enabled and select either the **Combo Box** or **List Box** control.

Step 7.	In the **Control Wizard**, choose to obtain values from a table or query, then select the table from the *other* side of the *many-to-many* join. In this case it's the *tblStaffInfo* table.
Step 8.	Select the primary key field from the table selected in Step 7 and select any additional fields which will assist in the identification of the correct record. In this case, the fields *ID, LastName,* and *FirstName* have been chosen.
Step 9.	Add any sorting order to your control. When prompted to adjust column width, you may wish to also enable **Hide Key Column**, since in most cases - including this example, the primary key contains unique but not useful data.
Step 10.	When prompted how to store the selected value, choose **Store that value in this field** and use the drop down box to select the foreign key field (you deleted its text box in Step 5).
Step 11.	It isn't necessary to provide a name for the control as the label for the deleted text box still exists. Complete the Wizard and delete the label associated with the new control.
Step 12.	Adjust the label **Caption** property for the former text box label to reflect the kind of data the new control will display (in this case *Staff Name*).
Step 13.	Open the form in **Form View** and test your work. You should be able to add new staff to an existing project, change an existing assignment from one staff member to another, and create a new project and populate it with staff members.

How to Manually Create a Data Entry Form Based on a Many-to-Many Join

The important task in the manual creation of such a form is the configuration of the **Combo** or **List Box** control. This procedure assumes that you have a form and subform using the same fields as described in the previous example.

Step 1.	Open your form and select the text box that is bound to the bridge table foreign key field (here it is the field *SID_FK*). Right click on the control and from the short cut menu, choose **Change To..**, then select either the **Combo Box** or the **List Box** control.
Step 2.	Open the **Property Sheet** for the control, move to the **Data** tab and select the **Builder (...)** associated with the **Row Source** property. The **Query Designer** will appear.
Step 3.	Use the **Show Table** dialog to add the table which represents the *other* table in the *many-to-many* join. Here it is the *tblStaffInfo* table.

Step 4.	Add the primary key and any other fields desired. This step maps to Step 8 in the previous procedure. Ensure that the primary key field is the first column.
Step 5.	Close the **Query Designer**. When prompted, indicate that you wish to save changes and update the property.
Step 6.	In the **Bound Column** property, ensure that the value is *1* (this maps to the column number where the primary key field from Step 4 is located).
Step 7.	Move to the **Format** tab. Adjust the **Column Count** property to equal the number of fields (hidden and unhidden) selected in Step 4.
Step 8.	Adjust the **Column Widths** property. For any column you wish to hide, indicate a width of *0″*. For multiple column controls, separate each width with a semicolon. Example, for a 3-column control with the first column hidden and the remaining columns at 1″ wide you specific the property as *0″; 1″; 1″*
Step 9.	Adjust the **List Width** property to equal the combined widths in the **Column Widths** property. Example from above: *2″*
Step 10.	Save the **Subform** and open the form in **Form Design View** to test your work. The functionality outlined in Step 13 from the previous procedure is a good test.

Troubleshooting Data Entry Using Forms Based on a Many-to-Many Join

The typical problem involves the incorrect identification of the foreign key field in the underlying bridge table.

- If you encounter an error that indicates that the field isn't editable it is usually because Access can't place data in one or both of the foreign key fields in the bridge table. Ensure that the subform's **Link Child Fields** is set to the main form's primary key (and that the **Link Master Fields** property correctly identifies the main form's primary key). Ensure that a control exists on the subform that is bound to the foreign key that maps to the primary key field in the other table participating in the *many-to-many* join.

- You get a parameter dialog box asking for a value. That indicates that a field name is spelled incorrectly. The dialog box will display the name of the field it is trying to resolve. Look for that field name spelling in the subform **Link Child** and **Link Master Fields** properties, as well as in the subform's **Record Source** property. Also investigate the **Row Source** property if you're using a **Combo** or **List Box** as outlined in the previous two examples.

Chapter 9 | Overview of Reports

Report Types

Reports are used to convey database information in a printed format. They share many design features with forms, but they are fundamentally different in that they may only be viewed. Users cannot interact with reports as they can with forms.

Like forms, reports may either be *bound* or *unbound* to an underlying record source. Subreports may be attached to *bound* reports to present related data (much in the way we've been working with subforms bound to forms), although this is not necessary to create *grouped* reports. Subreports may be used to display related data in a *one-to-many* or a *many-to-many* relationship, just as subforms do.

Beyond the fact that reports are essentially view-only and cannot respond to user interactions, reports include a feature not found in forms: grouping. Grouping is a powerful tool to bind information together. You can group on repeating data in a single table, or group on related data from two or more tables as if you were using a form/subform pair. In this way the use of subreports isn't as prominent as subforms are on forms.

Bound Reports

Bound reports are classified based on how they arrange data. The types of bound reports that you create either manually or by using a **Report Wizard** are outlined in the following table.

Bound Report Types

Report	Description
AutoReport	A quickly created report based on the currently selected table or query. Unless you need a printout of data in a hurry, using the **Report Wizard** to create any of the remaining bound report types is a better option.
Columnar	Lists fields and field labels as a single column running along the left side of the printed page.
Tabular	Presents field values in a grid, each column representing a field and each row representing field values from a record. This report type resembles a table, query, or form in **Datasheet View**.
Justified	Arranges field labels and controls so they span the full width of the report. A good option for records containing fields of the *Memo* data type.
Groups/Totals	The most common report type, related records are grouped or banded together (you can declare up to 10 grouping levels). When the **Report Wizard** is used and numeric or **Yes/No** fields are present, the wizard can create running sub and grand totals. The wizard also presents three options for arranging grouped data: *Stepped*, *Block*, and *Outline*.
Labels	Typically used for creating *mailing labels*. This report type uses a grid to group a cluster of field values. The clustered fields repeat across the page when printed. The layout of the grid depends upon the type of label stock you wish to use.

A Note on Groups/Totals Reports

Grouped reports can be based on a single table or on multiple tables. This capacity to group related data is different from the behavior of forms. For a form to display grouped data, you must use a **Subform Control** (or a wizard creates one for you) and the underlying record source is based on two or more related tables.

When a single table is used as the record source for a grouped report, you indicate the field or fields in the table that contain data you wish to group and a **Group Header** (and optionally a **Group Footer**) is created. For example, in a table containing staff information, you can group on a field named *Department*. By including staff *FirstName* and *LastName* fields, the report would group staff by department.

The components of a grouped report are discussed in detail in Chapter 10.

Unbound Reports

Unbound reports are used for many, unrelated purposes. Unbound reports fall into two general categories of use:

- Displaying data that are not related. By placing Subreport Controls on a report, you can embed existing reports within a larger report. These embedded reports will display their data independent of one another. The common thread is that the embedded reports are printed together along with any additional formatting you establish for the parent, unbound report.

- Creating auxiliary or support documents. You can create report covers, table of contents sheets, or other single or multiple-page documents. These can be inserted into bound reports if desired.

Report Views

We pick up an additional view while working with reports: **Print Preview**. The other report views offer the same functionality as similarly-named Form views. The **Print Preview** view displays the report as it will appear when printed.

You open the report in **Print Preview** in one of two ways: (1) when creating a report using the **Report Wizard** the default final step opens the report in **Print Preview**. Alternatively, when you open a report in **Report**, **Report Layout**, or **Report Design View**, you can select **Print Preview** by right-clicking on the report or by choosing the **View** command from the **Home** tab.

The **Print Preview** tab contains several groups, which are explained in the following table.

Print Preview Tab

Group	Description
Print	Opens the **Print** dialog box so you can select printers, set page ranges, copy numbers, etc.
Page Size	Select paper size, adjust margins, and elect to only print data (and not formatted elements).
Page Layout	Establish *Portrait* or *Landscape* page orientation and set the number of columns (the default is a single column).
Zoom	Determine the zoom level and number of pages to preview.
Data	Export the report data to another application or to a format such as RTF (Rich Text Format) or HTML.
Close	Close the **Print Preview** window (you may also right-click on the report and change views).

Creating an Auto Report

The simplest report is an **Auto Report**, created by using the **Report** button on the **Create** tab. This command creates a simple **Tabular** report and no care is taken to ensure that the data fit on the default page width. These reports are not grouped and there are no design choices offered, although once the report has been created you may make design and formatting changes by switching to either **Report Layout** or **Report Design View**.

How to Create an Auto Report

Step 1. Select a **Table** or **Query** from the **Navigation Pane** which will serve as the report data source.

Step 2. From the **Create** tab, in the **Reports** group, choose **Report**.

Step 3. The **Auto Report** will appear in **Report Layout View**.

Step 4. To save the report, select **Save** from the **Quick Access** toolbar, or when you close the report, choose **Yes** when prompted to save the report.

 If you were prompted to save the report when closing it, selecting *No* will abandon the design without saving it while selecting *Cancel* will return you to the current view of the report.

Creating a Simple Single-Table Report

This is the easiest type of report to create. Unlike creating an **Auto Report**, the **Report Wizard** offers an option to ensure that the controls all fit within a page width (for a new report this is determined by the default printer settings on the local computer).

How to Create a Single Table Report

Many of the dialog boxes for the **Report Wizard** resemble the **Form Wizard**. Where dialogs are different they are illustrated.

Step 1. From the **Create** tab, in the **Reports** group, choose **Report Wizard**.

Step 2. In the first dialog box, use the **Tables/Queries** drop down to choose the desired table or query for the report.

Step 3. Move the desired fields from the **Available Fields** list box to the **Selected Fields** list box, then choose **Next**.

Step 4. When prompted if you want to **Add any grouping levels**, skip this step by selecting **Next** (the following procedure will detail grouped reports). The third dialog box will appear similar to the following:

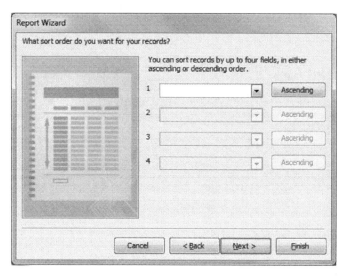

Step 5.   Select up to four sorting fields (for example, by *LastName* and then by *FirstName*. Choose **Next** when done. The next dialog box will appear similar to the following:

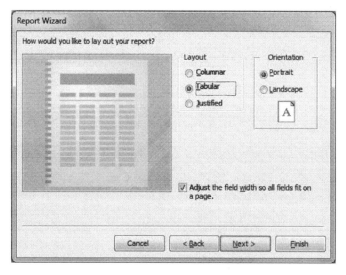

Step 6.   Choose a **Layout** (use the table on page 181 as a guide). It is strongly encouraged that you enable the **Adjust the field width** check box - otherwise the width of your report may spill across multiple pages. Choose a page **Orientation** as well. Choose **Next** when ready.

If your report contains more than roughly five or six text fields you may wish to choose the *Landscape* orientation. If fields appear truncated you may need to open the report in **Report Layout** or **Report Design View** and resize or move controls.

Step 7. Name the report using the final dialog box, then choose **Finish**. By default the report will open in **Preview View**. A simple report would appear similar to the following.

Staff

FirstName	LastName	Department	JobTitle	OfficeNumber
Amanda	Smith	Finance	Director	301
Robert	Jones	Finance	Analyst II	302
Tonya	Green	Finance	Analyst II	306
Michael	McDonald	Finance	Analyst III	310
Leon	DeLuca	IT	Programmer	B050
John	Michaels	IT	Programmer	B055

Single Table Grouped Reports

A grouped report may contain up to ten separate grouping levels. Each group is represented in the report as a **Group Header**. When you choose to group on a particular field, for example, by *Department* in a staff information table, the report will group staff by *department*. For reports that contain fields with numeric, currency or Yes/No data types, you can elect to add summary information to the report. If summary data are included, groups summarized will include a **Group Footer** as well. **Text Box** controls containing the summary functions will be located in the **Group Footer**. The detailed structure of a grouped report will be explored in Chapter 10.

How to Create a Simple Grouped Report

Step 1. From the **Create** tab, in the **Reports** group, choose **Report Wizard**.

Step 2. In the first dialog box, use the **Tables/Queries** drop down to choose the desired table or query for the report.

Step 3.   Move the desired fields from the **Available Fields** list box to the **Selected Fields** list box, then choose **Next**. The second dialog box of the **Report Wizard** will appear as follows:

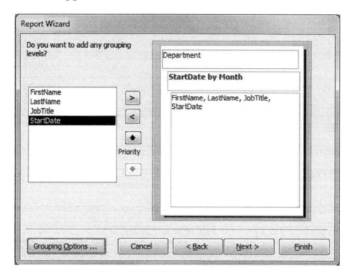

Step 4.   Add up to ten grouping levels. If desired, choose **Grouping Options** to control how a group is defined. Use the following table as a guide.

Grouping Options

Group Level Fields	Grouping Interval
Text	Group by entire field (as in *Dictionary order*) or by the first 1-5 characters.
Date/Time	Group normally (by exact date), or by larger units of time such as years, months, weeks, or unit of time.
Number	Group by value (normal method) or grouped into selected increments.

Step 5.   Once grouping has been established, choose **Next**. In the third dialog box, choose **Sort Order** for the *detail* records (for example, if grouping by *Department*, the staff *LastName* and *FirstName* fields will appear in the report's **Detail** area. In this example, sorting by *LastName* would be a good option.

Step 6.   If your report includes fields of a *number* data type, you may choose **Summary Options**. Any applied summary option will appear at the end of each group. Use the following table as a guide.

Summary Options

Group Level Fields	Grouping Interval
Summary Values	Apply any of the following operations: Sum, Average, or present the minimum and/or maximum value. These operations are applied at each detail level within a group.
Show	Sets whether the **Summary Values** appear at the end of each detail area or only at the group level.
Calculate Percent	If you choose to **Sum** any field(s), checking this control will calculate each sum (in detail or at the group level) as a percentage of the total (grand totals always appear at the end of a report).

Step 7. Choose **Next** once sorting options have been decided. In the next dialog box, select a **Layout** and page **Orientation**. Note that the **Layout** options are different now that the report has one or more grouping levels. Use the following table as a guide.

Grouping Layout Options

Option	Description
Stepped	Each group header appears on a separate line. If more than one group has been defined, each subgroup heading appears to the left of the parent group. Detail data occupy rows separate from any group headers. Column headers for the detail section appear at the top of each page.
Block	All group headers appear on the same line. Only detail data are indented. This creates the most compact report of the three options.
Outline	Similar to *Stepped* except the group and detail column headers repeat within the report body. This report consumes the most paper of the three report types.

Step 8. Once Layout and Orientation have been selected, choose **Next**. In the final **Report Wizard** dialog, name the report and choose **Finish**. A portion of a grouped report, grouped first by *Department* and then by year of hire (*StartDate*) appears below.

Staff by Department and Start Year					
Department	StartDate b	LastName	FirstName	OfficeNumber	JobTitle
Finance	2000	McDonald	Michael	310	Analyst III
	2005	Smith	Amanda	301	Director
	2007	Green	Tonya	306	Analyst II
		Jones	Robert	302	Analyst II
IT	2003	Michaels	John	B055	Programmer
	2004	Kidwell	Michael	B111	Director
	2005	DeLuca	Leon	B050	Programmer
	2007	Palmer	Susan	405	Webmaster
	2009	Jones	Jennifer	B012	Support Tech
	2010	Baseman	Tyrone	B408	Support Tech

Multiple Table Grouped Reports

When you use the **Report Wizard** and include two or more tables or queries as the report's record source, the wizard automatically suggests grouping levels as appropriate. You can override these suggested grouping levels or continue to add additional ones as desired. This is a useful feature, especially if you're new to banded or grouped reports as you can quickly revisit the Report Wizard and try another grouping pattern until you achieve the desired results.

As an example, consider the following relationship from a staff and projects database:

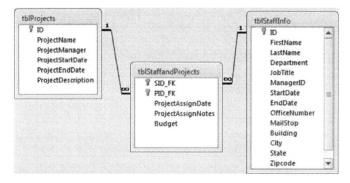

We'll use the **Report Wizard** to generate a report that, by *Department* and then by *ProjectName*, lists the staff and their assigned budgets. The report will total the budget for each project, and the total project budget assigned to each *Department*.

How to Create a Multiple Table Grouped Report

Step 1.   From the **Create** tab, in the **Reports** group, choose **Report Wizard**.

Step 2.   In the first dialog box, use the **Tables/Queries** drop down to choose the desired table or query for the report. This first table/query choice should represent data that serves as the report's top-level grouping.

Step 3.   Move the desired fields from the **Available Fields** list box to the **Selected Fields** list box.

Step 4.   Return to the **Tables/Queries** drop down box and select the next table or query, then move the desired fields from the **Available Fields** list box to the **Selected Fields** list box.

Step 5.   Repeat Step 4 as necessary until all table/queries and their associated fields have been added to the **Selected Fields** list box. Choose **Next** when done. For the purposes of this example, the following fields were selected (using the Staff and Projects database).

Table	Field
tblStaffInfo	Department, LastName, FirstName
tblProjects	ProjectName
tblStaffandProjects	Budget

The second dialog box of the **Report Wizard** appears similar to the following:

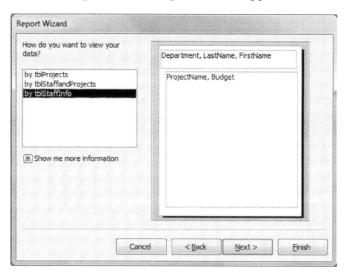

Step 6.   When working with multiple tables, the second dialog box is used to ensure that the top-most table/fields have been selected. In the illustration above it is verifying that our intent is to create a report that focuses on *Department*. If the top-level organization is not correct, choose the correct order from the **How do you want to view your data?** list box. Choose **Next** when ready.

Step 7.   In the third dialog box, select any grouping levels. In the examples illustrated here, we'd choose *Department* and then *ProjectName*. Note in the following illustration that the Wizard hasn't placed *ProjectName* correctly. Use the **Up** or **Down Priority** buttons to make adjustments. In this case, we'd move *ProjectName* up one level. If you need to adjust grouping options, choose the **Grouping Options** button and follow the discussion on page 186. Choose **Next** when ready.

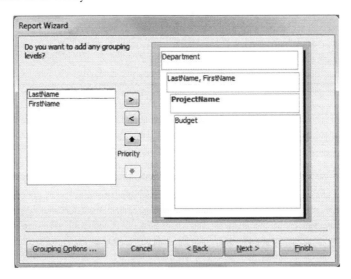

Step 8.   Select up to 4 sorting options in the fourth dialog box. Also use the **Summary Options** command to add any summary functions. In this example, we'd choose to sum on the *Budget* field and to accept the default value to show **Summary and Detail**. In this case it means that a running total will be created for each *ProjectName* and *Department* as well as a grand total for all project budgets. Choose **Next** when finished.

Step 9.   The fifth dialog box manages overall report layout. Choose a layout option and page orientation (use the discussion on page 187) as a guide. In this example, the report will be based on the **Block** layout style.

Step 10.   In the final dialog box enter a name for your report. When completed, the report will appear similar to the following.

C9_Department_ProjectBudget_Multiple			
Department	ProjectName	LastName	FirstName
Finance	Cloud Storage Implementation	McDonald	Michael

Summary for 'ID' = 11 (1 detail record)

		Budget	$7,500.00

Summary for 'ProjectName' = Cloud Storage Implementation (1 detail record)

		Project Total	$7,500.00
Finance	Financial System Reengineering	Smith	Amanda

Summary for 'ID' = 8 (1 detail record)

		Budget	$95,000.00
Finance	Financial System Reengineering	Jones	Robert

Summary for 'ID' = 9 (1 detail record)

		Budget	$1,000.00
Finance	Financial System Reengineering	McDonald	Michael

Summary for 'ID' = 11 (1 detail record)

		Budget	$1,000.00

Summary for 'ProjectName' = Financial System Reengineering (3 detail records)

		Project Total	$97,000.00

In the illustration above, a portion of the report details projects assigned to staff within the *Finance* department. Only one staff member, *Michael McDonald* was assigned to the *Cloud Storage Implementation* project, so both the staff and project total (of $7,500) are the same. The *Financial Systems Reengineering* project has three staff from the *Finance* department. Their individual budgets of *$95,000*, *$1,000*, and *$1,000* total to *$97,000* as detailed in the report. Further down in this multipage report are summary totals for each department, and at the bottom of the report is a grand total for all project budgets across all departments.

Creating Unbound Reports

An unbound report may be created by choosing to move into **Report Design** or selecting **Blank Report** from the **Reports** group on the **Create** tab. The difference between the two options is that the former choice places you in **Report Design View** while the latter opens a blank report in **Report Layout View**. In this procedure we'll outline opening a report in **Report Design View**.

How to Create an Unbound Report

Step 1.   From the **Reports** group on the **Create** tab, choose **Report Design**. A blank report, containing a **Detail** and **Page Header** and **Footer** will appear.

Step 2.   Add controls as necessary. You may wish to refer to the next chapter for details about the various report sections.

Step 3.   Save the report design by selecting **Save** from the **Quick Access** toolbar, or choose to save the report when prompted once you close the **Report Design View**.

Page Setup Properties

Report attributes such as page orientation, margins, paper source, and column formatting are manipulated by using the **Page Setup** tab. The page properties are stored separately for each report so you can create different report styles.

When you set or modify properties such as **Left** or **Right Margins**, Access does not adjust the report's **Width** property. If the combined total of the left and right margins and the report **Width** (which corresponds to the region *between* the margins) exceeds the physical width of the page, Access may crop some portions of the report and spill those over to an additional page to the right.

The **Page Setup** tab is available when in **Report Layout** or **Report Design View**. Additionally, many of the controls on this tab are available when viewing the report in **Print Preview**.

How to Modify Page Setup Properties

Step 1.   Open the desired report in either **Report Layout** or **Report Design View**.

Step 2.   Select the **Page Setup** tab. The following table outlines the controls available from this tab.

Page Setup Tab

Command	Description
Page	Select from a list of predefined US and International paper and envelope standards.
Margins	Choose from a gallery of predefined margin combinations. Margins may be customized using the **Page Setup** command.
Show Margins	Display the effect of margins when viewing the report in **Report Layout**
Print Data Only	Omit formatted elements and only print the contents of bound controls.
Portrait/Landscape	Select portrait or landscape orientation for the current paper selection.
Columns	Create a multi-column report - these controls are part of the **Page Setup** dialog box.
Page Setup	Manages all of the options above plus provides the ability to select a printer, and if supported, a specific paper tray.

Step 3.   For quick adjustments, use any of the controls available from the **Page Size** or **Page Layout** group. For detailed adjustments, open the **Page Setup** dialog box. If you open the **Page Setup** dialog, the three tabs on this control are further explained below.

Page Setup Dialog

Tab	Option	Description
Page Setup	Margins	Sets the **Top**, **Left, Right**, and **Bottom** margins for the page. Measurement units displayed correspond to the **International Settings** of the computer.
	Print Data Only	Displays only field values on the report or form when checked. All other objects such as labels, lines, and images are rendered invisible (although they are still part of the report or form design).
	Split Form	If the selected object is a **Split Form** you may elect to print only the form or only the datasheet component.
Page	Orientation	Specifies whether the report will print in **Portrait** or **Landscape** orientation.
	Paper	Controls the **Paper Size** and the paper **Source**. The latter option refers to printer-specific paper trays or manual feed options.
	Printer for *Report Name*	Indicates whether the report will use the **Default Printer** (as specified by the computer's **Printer Settings**), or a **Specific Printer** available to the computer. In the latter case, use the **Printer** button to select the alternate printer.
Column	Grid Settings	Controls grid attributes for **Column** reports. If the **Number of Columns** is 2 or greater, you can set specific **Row Spacing** and **Column Spacing** values. Note that generally **Row Spacing** is not required, as spacing in the report's **Detail** section will keep records apart vertically. The **Column Spacing** controls the *gutter* or non-printing space between columns.
	Column Size	Controls the **Width** and **Height** settings for the column. If the **Same as Detail** option is checked (the default and preferred setting), the column's size settings are based on the size of the report's **Detail** section. If you elect to work with settings which are not the same as the detail section's, note that the **Width** and **Height** values may not exceed those of the **Detail** section's settings.
	Column Layout	Specifies the order used to print records across the page.

Step 4.   Adjust **Page Setup** properties as desired.

Step 5.   Choose **OK**.

Page Setup properties are stored with the current report (or form), but are not available through the **Property Sheet** for the report. When you alter any **Page Setup** properties, you will be prompted to save the report design when you close the report in **Report Design View** or **Print Preview**.

Troubleshooting Reports

Reports are generally prone to the same general errors that you may encounter when working with forms. For example, on either a form or a report, a calculated control that contains a syntax error in its **Control Source** property will display the expression **#NAME?** or **#ERROR?** warning. If you notice such content, especially in a **Text Box** control, review the **Control Source** property to ensure that there are no syntax errors.

The most common problem with reports is associated with the fact that, unlike forms, a report's width (a combination of the **Detail** section **Width** property plus the right and left margin settings in the **Page Setup** dialog) is linked to a physical object: the printed output. If a single control is accidentally moved just a bit too much to the right while in **Report Layout** or **Report Design View** Access will automatically increase the size of the **Detail** section's **Width** property to accommodate the "change". When you view the altered report in **Print Preview** or send the report to a printer, you'll notice alternating blank pages or alternating pages that print a small amount of information.

This problem is automatically generated if you use the **Quick Report** feature on a table that contains more than a page width worth of fields. You can see this behavior by clicking once on a multi-field table then choosing **Report** from the **Reports** group on the **Create** tab. When you print preview the report you'll notice that rather than try to fit the table contents in columns on a single page, Access will let fields spill across to additional pages, resulting in a printed report that may be more than one physical page wide.

How to Troubleshoot Excessively Wide Reports

Use these tips to help keep your reports to the width of a printed page.

- If data spills across to a second page (usually when a report is created using the **Quick Report** feature), you may need to spend time in **Report Design View** to reorder controls on the report. Note the left and right margin settings in the **Page Setup** dialog and the physical width of the paper you intend to use. The physical page width minus both margin settings will yield the value to use for the report **Detail** section's **Width** property. Note that value and move all controls (including any **Line** controls) so they are fully to the left of the correct **Detail** sections calculated width (use the ruler at the top of **Report Design View**). Once all controls are within the correct area, move the right side of the **Detail** section (or adjust its **Width** property) and view the report in **Print Preview**.

- If only a small portion of a line or control crosses over to the next page you should locate that control and make adjustments on it. One way to accomplish this is to open the report in **Report Design View** and note where along the horizontal ruler the **Detail** section ends. As above, that value must equal or be less than the physical page width minus both right and left page margins. If it isn't, move the mouse over the ruler until it changes to a downward-pointing arrow. Click just to the left of the end of the **Detail** section, which will select any controls which are at the edge of the **Detail** section (this procedure is discussed beginning on page 68). Move or shorten the control or controls which have been selected, then move the **Detail** section (or adjust its **Width** property) so it, plus page left and right margins, become equal to, or are less than the width of the physical page. Again, move to **Print Preview** to ensure proper behavior.

Chapter 10 | Report Design View

Report Design vs. Report Layout Views

As discussed in Chapter 9, of the two design views available when working with reports, **Report Design View** is preferred for serious report development. Both offer sets of report and page setup tools, but **Report Design View** offers more technical control over the formatting of your report.

Because **Layout** view has restrictions on important design activities and all of these features are available through the standard **Report Design** view, this book will focus on the more powerful design mode and allow the reader to explore the limited subset of design tools available through **Report Layout** view. It may initially seem like a limitation that you can't design a form and see the data displayed on the form at the same time, but the far richer set of controls, properties, and design tools available through the design view makes up for the deficiency of seeing data in real time.

Tabs Associated with Report Design View

The following tables outline the three tabs available when working in **Form Design View**.

Design Tab

Group	Description
Views	Switch between Report, Preview, Layout, and Design views.
Themes	Select predefined or custom themes, color groups, and/or font groups. These options are discussed in more detail later in this chapter.
Grouping & Totals	Control grouping, summaries, and the visibility of *detail* records.
Controls	Displays a palette of bound and unbound controls which may be placed on a form. Also add additional ActiveX controls. Controls are discussed in detail in Chapter 5. Specifically, report controls are discussed in Chapter 12.
Header/Footer	Add a title, logo, or a date/time text box to a form.
Tools	Manages the visibility of the properties, field list, and tab order windows. Opens a subform in a separate window, and opens the VBA code editor.

Arrange Tab

Name	Description
Table	Tools for working with table layouts, which cluster controls on a report. **Table Layouts** may be applied and removed. They are added by default to forms created using the **Report** control in the **Create** group. Table layouts are not created by default when a form is created using the **Report Wizard** or when building a form from scratch.
Rows & Columns	Tools for modifying and arranging rows and columns when working with a Table Layout. These controls are not available unless a **Table Layout** is present and selected on a report.
Merge / Split	Merges or splits controls within a **Table Layout**. Not available unless a **Table Layout** is present and selected.
Move	Moves the selected control or controls within the detail area of the report or between the detail area and the report header and footer. Only available when working with controls contained within a **Table Layout**.
Position	Sets margins, padding, and anchoring for controls contained within a **Table Layout**.
Sizing & Ordering	Sets various sizing, positioning, alignment, and *Z-order* (front/back) placements for one or more controls. These powerful tools are discussed in detail in Chapter 5 as they perform the same functions between forms and reports.

Format Tab

Name	Description
Selection	Choose a specific control or all controls on the report (there are also methods available using the mouse and keyboard to select one or more controls - see Chapter 5).
Font	Set font attributes, and text alignment for text-based controls. The **Format Painter** is also available which permits quick copy of a broad array of formatting attributes between controls.
Number	Apply predefined format attributes to numeric, currency, and date-based fields.
Background	Apply a background graphic or set alternating row colors (if the report has records in the **Detail** section.
Control Formatting	Apply predefined styles and shapes to certain controls (for example, command buttons and tab controls), define conditional formatting (mainly to text-based controls), and choose fill colors, control shapes, and special effects (depending upon the control type, some tools are not available).

Sections of a Report

Reports may consist of several sections including a detail section (mandatory), and report, page, and group headers and footers. With the exception of the detail section, all other sections are optional and may be added or removed easily.

Points on Report Sections

- All reports have at a minimum a detail section and the report object itself. All other sections are optional.

- The detail section displays the values of individual records. For grouped reports, the bound controls in the detail section constitute field values for records at the innermost grouping level.

- Headers and Footers for groups, pages, or reports may or may not be paired. For any Header or Footer, you can elect to display Header only, Footer only, or both.

- Group Headers and Footers can contain bound controls that respond to field values for the current grouping level. Example: In a report which groups employees by Department, a control bound to the Department field and contained within the Department group Header will display the name of each department on the report only once. The bound controls in the Detail section will print once for each employee record within the Department group.

- Group Headers or Footers are excellent locations for calculated controls to sum data from the **Detail** section. Once a report is rendered, either in **Report** or **Print Preview** views, the headers and footers for a group "see" all of the detail controls within that group, thus making subtotals and counts possible.

- Page Headers and Footers appear only once per page, at either the top or the bottom of the printed page.

- Report Headers and Footers appear only once per report, as either the first or last section to be printed on the report.

Adding and removing **Report** and **Page** headers and footers is discussed on page 203. Adding and removing **Group Headers** and **Footers** is discussed on page 232.

Report Sections, Data, and Printed Report

Structure of a Simple Report

A report created without any grouping levels but with report and page headers and footers would consist of five sections:

- The Report Header will be the first section to print on the report. It only appears once, at the top of the first page of the report.

- The Page Header will print next, and each time the report requires another sheet of paper.

- The Detail section will print continuously until all the records in the recordset have been printed. The only interruption will be the inclusion of a Page Footer at the end of a printed page (in a multiple-page report) and a Page Header at the top of the next page. After formatting and printing the Page Header on a subsequent page, the Detail section will continue printing.

- Page Footers will appear at the bottom of each printed page.

- The Report Footer will print following completion of the Detail section. It only appears once, toward the end of the last printed page. The last item printed on the final page of the report will be another Page Footer.

A simple report, using fields such as *FirstName, LastName, Office, OfficePhone,* and *Department* and appearing without any grouping levels, would appear in **Report Design View** similar to the following (note how similar this view is to a form in **Form Design View**).

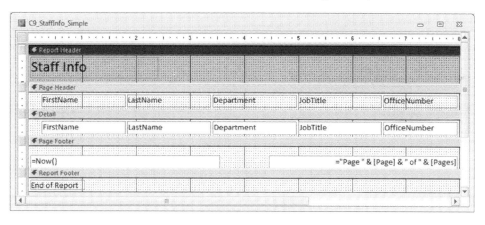

The top of the first page of this simple report, when viewed in the **Print Preview** window, would appear similar to the following:

Staff Info

FirstName	LastName	Department	JobTitle	OfficeNumber
Amanda	Smith	Finance	Director	301
Robert	Jones	Finance	Analyst II	302
Tonya	Green	Finance	Analyst II	306
Michael	McDonald	Finance	Analyst III	310
Leon	DeLuca	IT	Programmer	B050
John	Michaels	IT	Programmer	B055
Susan	Palmer	IT	Webmaster	405

The bottom of the last page of this simple report would appear similar to the following:

Lauren	De Haven	Marketing	Director	810
John	Link	Marketing	Sales Rep	100-A
Leslie	Morgan	Marketing	Sales Rep	100-D
Alicia	Wu	Marketing	Sales Rep	100-B
Margaret	Rosa	Marketing	Customer Care	110

End of Report

Tuesday, July 23, 2013   Page 1 of 1

Structure of a Grouped Report

A report created with two grouping levels, containing a **Group Header** and **Group Footer**, and with report and page headers and footers, would consist of nine sections: As an example of how these report sections interact, consider the following example. We'll borrow from the concepts laid down in the discussion of grouped reports with multiple tables, presented on page 188

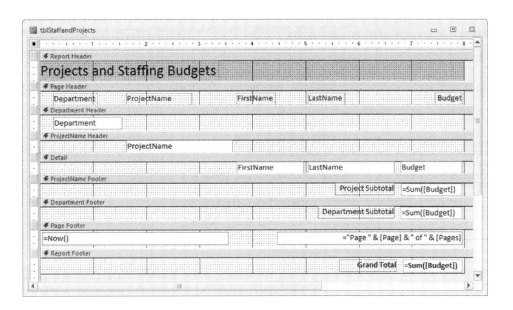

Section	Behavior When Printed
Report Header	The content in this section prints once, at the top of the first page on a report. This is an optional section.
Page Header	Any controls present in a **Page Header** print once at the top of each page. Despite its name, if a **Report Header** is present the **Page Header** prints *after* the **Report Header**. An optional section on a report.
Department Header	This is one of two group headers on this report (a report may contain up to ten grouping levels). The contents in this section print once at the beginning of each new group item, in this case, for each *Department* contained in the report's **Record Source**. Groups are optional.
ProjectName Header	The second of two group headers on this report. Within each *Department*, the contents of this section print once for each separate *ProjectName* associated with the current *Department*.
Detail	This mandatory report section (the only one that is mandatory) contains the controls that detail the lowest level of organized data. Because this sample report focuses on staff budgets by *ProjectName* and then by *Department* this section prints the detail data (Staff name and *Budget*) for each project and department. The detail section may be interrupted if it gets close to the bottom of the printed page in which a **Page Footer**, and on the following page, a **Page Header** are inserted. Until the detail records are exhausted, this section continues to print.
ProjectName Footer	The contents of this group footer print once upon completion of any detail data associated with the current *ProjectName*. The report increments to the next *ProjectName* for the current *Department* if applicable, otherwise the next section also prints. A group footer, which is optional, is a great location for summary data such as subtotals. In this sample report, a calculated control is present that sums budget by *ProjectName* within each *Department*.
Department Footer	Similar to the previous section but prints upon the completion of all *ProjectName* and **Detail** data for the current project. The report increments to the next *Department*, or if none exist, prints the next two sections. A good location for summary data at, in this case, the *Department* level. In the sample report a calculated control totals all project budget data for the current *Department*.
Page Footer	Prints once at the end of each page so this section is a good choice for running footers that may display page numbering. **Page footers** are optional.
Report Footer	Prints upon completion of the report but unlike the **Report Header**, this section prints *before* the **Page Footer** (if present). This section "sees" all of the report data (as does the **Report Header**) and is a great place to provide grand total or grand summary data. In the sample report a calculated control tallies all project budgets for all departments. This section is optional.

Report or **Page Headers** and **Footers** need not be paired. See the following section for details.

How to Add or Remove the Report or Page Headers and Footers

If you remove a header or footer section that contains controls, the controls will be permanently removed from the report. You can, however, adjust the **Height** property of a header or footer to 0. Note that if the section contains controls, their **Height** property must also be set to zero and they must be aligned at the top of the section. Although the header or footer will not appear on the report, the controls it contains are still contained within that section The report must be open in **Report Design View.**

Step 1.   Right click anywhere in the **Detail** section but not on an existing control. Alternatively you can right click on the **Detail** bar above the **Detail** section.

Step 2.   From the short cut menu, choose either **Report Header/Footer** or **Page Header/Footer**.

If you intend to add a **Report Header** that contains a logo or a title, you can also select **Logo** or **Title** from the **Header/Footer** group on the **Design** tab.

If you intend to *add* a **Page Header** or **Footer** that contains a page number or the report print date, you can also select **Page Numbers** or **Date and Time** from the **Header/Footer** group on the **Design** tab. A dialog box will appear that lets you select format and header or footer location.

How to Remove an Individual Report or Page Header or Footer

Step 1.   Position the mouse pointer at the lowest portion of the section to remove.

Step 2.   When the mouse pointer appears as a cross-shaped up- and down-pointing arrow, click and drag the section upward until it no longer appears.

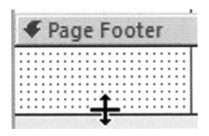

 You can also remove a **Report** or **Page Header** or **Footer** by setting the appropriate section's **Height** property to *0* using the **Property Sheet**. If the section contains controls, these must also have their **Height** property set to zero (or be removed from the section) before the section's **Height** can be set to zero.

Report Properties

Report or control properties set or describe an attribute of a report or control. Many properties can be changed while a few are *read-only* and cannot be changed by the report designer. Examples of common properties that can readily be changed include the report's **Width** property, which controls the width of the printed portion of the report between the **Right** and **Left** margins.

Reports have fewer properties than forms (about 50 as opposed to nearly 70 for forms) since they serve only to display data. As with forms, reports have a few commonly used properties that developers use frequently.

All report properties are set by using the **Property Sheet**, or for common format properties, by using the **Format** tab.

How to Change a Report Property

Step 1.   Double-click on the **Report Selector**, or on the **Design** tab, in the **Tools** group, select **Property Sheet**. A property sheet similar to the following will appear:

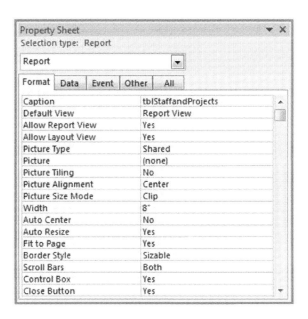

Property Sheet Category Tabs

Tab	Description
Format	Lists properties that affect the visual appearance of the report.
Data	Displays properties that control how the report interacts with its underlying record source. Unbound reports will have this category of properties, although some entries will be blank.
Event	Lists *events* that the report can respond to. An event is some action, elicited by either the user or by the database. Reports cannot respond to *user events* like forms. A report can only respond to *internal events*. Events are handled by using *macros* or by writing VBA procedures.
Other	Lists properties that do not readily fall into the above-listed categories.
All	Displays all properties in a single list.

Step 2.   Select the desired **Category Tab**.

Step 3.   Select the text box for the desired property.

Step 4.   Type a new property value, or select a new property value from the drop-down list, or select the **Builder (...)** and use it to create a new property value.

Common Report Format Properties

Option	Description
Caption	Sets the text that appears on the report's **Title bar** when viewed in the **Print Preview** window.
Default View	Sets the default opening view - either **Report** or **Print Preview**.
Picture	Specifies the name of the graphic file for the report's background image.
Picture Type	Indicates whether the picture is *Embedded* (default) or *Linked* to a file.
Picture Alignment	Controls how the picture is aligned within the report when pictures smaller than the report body.
Picture Tiling	Specifies whether to use a single copy of the picture (*No*) or to tile the picture for pictures smaller than the report body. The default is *No*.
Width	Controls the width of the report body. The sum of the width and the **Left** and **Right Margins** must not exceed the width of the physical page. When this happens, Access will insert extra pages and print the excess width on them.
Grp Keep Together	Specifies how groups are kept together on a report. The options are *By Page* or *By Column* (default).
Picture Pages	Specifies whether the picture is to appear on every page or just the first page.
Page Header	Controls whether a **Page Header** is printed on the same page as the **Report Header**.
Page Footer	Controls whether a **Page Footer** is printed on the same page as the **Report Footer**.
Layout for Print	Specified whether to use printer fonts (*Yes*) or screen fonts (*No*). The default is *Yes*.

Common Report Data Properties

Property	Description
Record Source	Specifies the report's record source. If the record source is a table or a named query the object's name is displayed. If the record source is an SQL statement, the statement is displayed. You can evoke a **Builder** to create or modify an SQL statement for the record source.
Filter	Specifies the filter conditions for the report. Generally a report inherits a filter from a table or query.
Filter On Load	Controls whether the report opens and applies the filter. The default is *Off*.
Order By	Controls how the recordset data are ordered. Generally report's can inherit an *Order* from a table or query, or the property can be set via a VBA procedure or a macro.
Order By On Load	Controls whether report orders or sorts data. The default is *Off*.

Common Report Events

Event	Description
On Open	Triggered when the Report is opened, but immediately before it appears in the **Print Preview** window or is sent to the printer.
On Close	Triggered when the form is closed, and removed from the screen, or when printing is completed.
On No Data	Triggered when a report is opened but there are no records to display.

Event processing requires a macro or VBA code. The property's text box displays either the name of a macro or the term *Event Procedure* depending upon whether a macro or a VBA procedure is attached, respectively

Event processing is covered in the book *Building VBA Apps using Microsoft Access*, which is part of this series.

Common Other Report Properties

Property	Description
Date Grouping	Controls whether the first day of the week and the first day of the year are set using *U.S. Settings* or *System Settings* (default). System settings are obtained from the *International Settings* in the **Control Panel.** Note that the **Control Panel** is a Microsoft Windows object.
Ribbon Name	The name of a custom ribbon to open when the report is opened.
Menu Bar	Specifies a custom menu bar to be used in lieu of the standard Access menu bar.
Toolbar	Specifies a custom toolbar to be used in lieu of the standard toolbars.
Shortcut Menu Bar	Controls whether the user can open a shortcut menu by right-clicking on the report in **Print Preview**.
Fast Laser Printing	Optimizes printing of lines when using a laser printer. If you require overlapping graphic elements on a report, set this property to *No*

Chapter 11 | Data-Bound Reports

A bound report is a report that is connected to an underlying **Record Source** - usually either a table or a query based on one or more tables. Like bound forms, a bound report contains controls that display the underlying data. Also like forms, the most common bound control on a bound report is the **Text Box.**

Although forms and reports are fundamentally different, when in **Layout** or **Design View** the techniques for placing, arranging, modifying, and adjusting properties of the various bound and unbound controls are identical. In various sections in this chapter we'll refer to previous discussion of form controls where appropriate. The chapter following this one deals with report controls but only as they specifically relate to the unique properties of a report.

Points on Bound Reports

- When you create a report that is based on a single table, the report is bound to that table. This is true regardless of whether you create the report yourself or use the Report Wizard.

- When working with reports that display data from two or more tables related in a many-to-many join, the report's record source must be based on a query or an SQL statement. Report Wizards build these SQL statements automatically.

- Reports which display data from two or more tables related in a one-to-many join use groups, rather than subreports, to display the related data. Data from the one side of the join will usually supply information for one or more groups and the data from the table on the many side of the join will supply data for the report's **Detail** section. You can define up to ten grouping levels.

- Regardless of the nature of the record source, all the fields in the record source are available to the report via the Field List. In **Report Design View** you can add or remove bound controls and therefore control which fields are displayed.

- Bound reports can contain both bound and unbound controls. In addition, there are a number of Control Wizards that make working with controls easier.

- If a report uses a query as its record source and you modify the query to add or remove fields, the list of fields available to the report in **Report Design View** also changes. Removing a field from a query used by a report will not automatically remove the corresponding bound control from the report. You must remove the control manually.

- Reports are sensitive to width since ultimately their output is intended for the physical page. The **Report Wizard** may not do an adequate job of sizing and/or spacing controls and frequently a developer will spend time making adjustments to ensure that the report formats correctly when sent to a printer.

Bound Reports and Bound Controls

If a bound report is in **Report Layout** or **Report Design View**, you can review the list of available fields by displaying the **Field List**. Any field dragged from this list onto the report becomes a *bound control*. Although the most common control type is a **Text Box**, Access determines the type of control created depending upon the field's data type. For example, inserting a field of the *Yes/No* data type will typically create a **Check Box** control, while inserting a field of the *OLE Object* data type will insert a **Bound Object Frame** control.

Controls that can display text will show the name of the bound field when viewed in report **Design View**. An example of a text box control bound to a field is illustrated below.

Properties Controlling Bound Reports and Controls

Object	Properties
Report	The **Record Source** property names the table or query or displays the *SQL statement* that is used to provide the records for the report.
Control	The **Control Source** property lists the field from the report's **Record Source** that the control is bound to.
Subform or Subreport	The **Source Object** names the report contained by the **Subform/Subreport** control.
	The **Link Master Fields** property lists the fields that constitute the primary key in the relationship join.
	Link Child Fields property lists the foreign key fields in the relationship join.

How to View the Field List

The field list is only available when the report is in **Report Layout** or **Report Design View**.

Step 1.   On the **Design** tab, in the **Tools** group, choose **Add Existing Fields**.

The **Field List** is illustrated on page 51.

How to Modify a Report's Record Source

Use this procedure to change the table, query or SQL statement that specifies the report's record source. This procedure would generally be conducted if you need to add additional fields to the record source.

Step 1.   Open the **Property Sheet** by double-clicking on the report **Selector**, or if the **Property Sheet** is open, ensure that it is displaying properties for the report by single-clicking on the report **Selector** (this control is analogous to the **Form Selector**).

Step 2.   In the **Property Sheet**, select the **Data** tab.

Step 3.   Select the text box that corresponds to the **Record Source** property.

Step 4.   If you wish to change the **Record Source** to an existing table or query, select the new **Record Source** from the drop-down list. This action would end the procedure. Alternatively, to modify an existing SQL statement or to create a new SQL statement, select the **Builder**.

Step 5.   If the **Record Source** was formerly a table, you will be prompted as to whether you wish to create a query based on the table. Choose **Yes**.

Step 6.   In the **Query Builder**, add or remove fields and/or tables as desired.

Step 7.   Close the **Query Builder** when done. A dialog box similar to the following will appear:

Step 8.   Choose **Yes** to save the query as an SQL statement for the report's **Record Source** property, or choose **No** to abandon changes to the report's **Record Source** property, or choose **Cancel** to return to the **Query Builder**.

If you save the query from within the **Query Builder**, it becomes a named query and will appear in the list of queries in the **Database Window**.

SQL statements generated by the **Query Builder** may contain *criteria expressions* and specify *sort orders*.

How to Add a Field to a Report

Step 1.   Ensure that the desired field is visible from the **Field List** (if not, see the previous procedure).

Step 2.   Use the mouse to drag the field to the desired section of the report and release the mouse when done.

Step 3.   Adjust the control's position, size and design properties as desired. These adjustments are discussed in Lesson 5.

You can drag several fields from the **Field List** at once. To select multiple contigious fields, hold down the *Shift* key while selecting the fields. To select multiple, non-contigious fields, hold down the *Ctrl* key while selecting fields. When done, drag any selected field onto the report and release.

How to Delete a Bound Control

Step 1.   If the report is not in **Report Design View**, change to that view.

Step 2.   Select the desired control by clicking once on it. Selection rectangles will appear indicating that the control has been selected.

Step 3.   Press the *Delete* **key.**

To immediately undo a control deletion, press *Ctrl* + z.

How to Change a Bound Control's Control Source Property

By changing the **Control Source** property you change the field the control is bound to.

Step 1.   Select the desired control.

Step 2.   Display the **Property Sheet** if necessary.

Step 3.   On the **Property Sheet**, select the **Data** tab.

Step 4.   Select the text box associated with the **Control Source** property.

Step 5.   Select another field from the drop-down list.

How to Save a Report Design

Whenever you modify the design of a report and attempt to close either the report **Design View** or any of the other report views, you will be prompted to save changes to the report design.

Step 1.   From the **Quick Access** toolbar, choose **Save**. Alternatively, choose to save the report design when prompted if you close a report that has been modified.

Chapter 12 | Report Controls

Overview of Report Controls

Controls on reports are used to display data or provide for report formatting. Like forms, reports can contain both bound and unbound controls, the latter being used as *calculated controls*, and in the case of lines and rectangles, as graphic elements.

Although the **Control Toolbox** in **Report Design View** is identical to that in **Form Design View**, many of the controls will not function, or are out of context on a report. This is because the user cannot interact with a report.

Controls, like reports, have properties that specify or control important formatting, data, and usability attributes. The **Property Sheet** will display the properties for the currently selected control on a report. For controls that display text, such as labels and text boxes, you can also adjust formatting properties by using the **Formatting toolbar.**

The most commonly used controls on reports include text boxes, line and rectangle control and image controls. The controls which indicate Yes/No status (option button, check box and toggle button) will correctly indicate the Yes/True/On or No/False/Off state of a field value, but obviously cannot interact in the same manner as they can when placed on a form. The remaining controls generally are not used as they are intended to serve as user interface objects and lack the ability to interact with the user when placed on a report. For example, a **Combo Box** control is out of context on a report, as is a **Command Button**. The following table lists the most useful controls for Reports.

The controls discussed in this chapter have unique properties or features when used in reports. For discussion of all other controls, refer to Chapter 5, beginning on page 56.

Useful Report Controls

Control	Description
Text Box	Display of text, memo, and all numeric data types.
Label	Label other controls, column headings, other report regions.
Page Break	Create a page break for **Print Preview** and printed output.
Chart	Format numeric data graphically.
Line/Rectangle	Provides organization to areas of the report.
Check Box	Displays Yes/True/On or No/False/Off data graphically.
Unbound Object Frame	Useful for adding images or graphics which are not bound.
Option Button	Similar to the Check Box control.
Subform/Subreport	Generally used to contain groups of unrelated data or when a report is bound and grouped to several related tables.
Bound Object Frame	Displays graphic data which is bound.
Image Control	Displays a static graphic such as a watermark or a logo.

Bound and Unbound Controls

Generally, dragging fields from the Field List creates bound controls, and unbound controls are created by working with the appropriate control tool from the **Control Toolbar**. Bound controls that display text will show the name of the field they are bound to. Similar controls that are unbound will display the text *Unbound*. Unbound **Text Box** controls are generally used as *calculated controls* on a report.

Points on Bound and Unbound Controls

- You can bind an unbound control created by using a control tool on the Control group by modifying the control's **Field Source** property.

- Although you can unbind a bound control (you may wish to convert the control into a calculated control), this is not recommended. Access stores information about the binding that cannot be altered by the developer. It is best to create a new unbound control of the appropriate type by using a control tool from the Control Toolbar.

- If the report's **Record Source** property is modified and a field is removed, the bound control for that field will display and/or print the message **#Name?** You should either delete the control or modify its Field Source property to bind it to another field.

How to Add a Bound Control from the Field List

Most fields will create a **Text Box** when dragged onto a report. Fields with some data types such as Yes/No or OLE Object will create **Check Box** or **Bound Object Frames**, respectively. Note that controls can be changed into other control types. This is discussed on page 80.

Step 1.   Ensure that the desired field is visible from the **Field List**.

Step 2.   Use the mouse to drag the field to the desired section of the report and release the mouse when done.

Step 3.   Adjust the control's position, size, and design properties as desired. These adjustments are discussed beginning on page 69.

Common Control Properties

Controls have fewer properties than reports, and the number of properties associated with a control varies between control types. For example, the **Label** control has no **Data** properties at all, reflecting the fact that labels cannot be bound.

When you modify a control's formatting attributes by using the **Format** tab, the **Property Sheet** is automatically updated. For controls that display text, entering **Edit Mode** in order to enter or edit text blocks the ability to modify format properties. You must first exit edit mode before making format property adjustments.

Like with form controls, report controls have commonly used properties. These are detailed in the following tables.

Common Control Format Properties

Property	Description
Caption	Sets the display text for controls such as labels and command buttons.
Width	Specifies the control's width.
Height	Specifies the control's height.
Visible	Controls whether a control is visible.
Left	Indicates the position of the left side of the control relative to the upper left corner of the report. You can express the values in any common unit of measurement, e.g., *0.2 in* or *34 cm*.
Top	Indicates the position of the top of the control relative to the upper left corner of the report. Units are the same as for the **Left** property.
Back Style	Controls whether the background in the control is transparent or not (*Normal*). Normal is the default.
Back Color	Sets the color of the control background, which is only available if the **Back Style** property is set to *Normal*.
Special Effect	Specifies whether the control has any special effects such as raised, sunken, or etched. The default value varies between control types.
Border Style	Controls the style of the borderline around a control.
Border Width	Sets the width of the borderline.
Border Color	Sets the color of the borderline.
Fore Color	Controls the font color for controls that display text.
Font Name	Sets the font for controls that display text.
Font Size	Specifies the font size for controls that display text.
Font Weight	Sets the font weight (thickness of the characters) for controls that display text. The **Bold** value is analogous to applying the **Bold** font attribute to the text.
Font Italic	Sets *Italic* on or off for controls which display text.
Font Underline	Sets <u>Underline</u> on or off for controls which display text.
Can Grow	Enables a control or a report **Section** to increase height automatically in order to accommodate content. Generally you should enable this property both for the control of interest and for its containing **Section**.
Can Shrink	Enables a control or a report **Section** to decrease height automatically to accommodate the lack of content. As with **Can Grow**, it's best to set this property both for the controls within a section and the section itself.

Common Control Data Properties

Property	Description
Control Source	Indicates the field that the control is bound to. If blank, the control is unbound.
Running Sum	Controls whether a text box can calculate running totals beyond the context of a group. The choices are *No* (default), *Over Group* or *Over All*. In the latter cases, the text box will retain totals across all accumulated groups, or across the entire report, respectively. This property is only available to text boxes on reports.

Common Control Other Properties

Property	Description
Name	Sets the name of the control. This is different from the **Caption** property of controls. Most developers name controls in a manner reflecting their function. Example: a text box that sums *Hotel* costs would be named *txtSumofHotel*.
Vertical	For **Text Box** and **Label** controls, sets whether the display text is aligned horizontally (*No*) or vertically (*Yes*). The default is *No*. This does not rotate the control, only the display text.

Many controls present properties that have no meaning on a report. For example, all report controls have a **Tab Stop** and **Tab Index** property. Although you can tab through report controls in **Report Layout View**, setting these properties has no real functional effect.

Report Controls and the Control Wizard

Chapter 5 discussed those form controls that are associated with a **Control Wizard**. Only a subset of those form controls have a wizard for report controls. These being **Option Group, Combo Box, Chart, List Box**, and **Subreport**. Of these, the **Combo** and **List Box Wizards** aren't particularly useful as these controls may only display data when the report is opened. When a report is opened in **Report Layout View** you can manipulate these controls but the action has no effect.

There are report controls that do have meaningful control wizards. The **Chart** and **Subreport** controls each provide a wizard that assists in the creation of a useful control (in the case of the **Chart** control the wizard is evoked regardless of the state of the **Use Control Wizards** option).

Using the **Chart** control is discussed beginning on page 143 and it's use on a report is similar to how it is used on a form. The **Subreport** control is the report analog to the **Subform** control for forms. Use of this wizard (for **Subforms**) is discussed beginning on page 110.

Manually Working with Report Controls

The majority of controls on the **Control Toolbox** lack **Control Wizards**. Regardless of the control type, there is a generalized procedure for working with a control without the assistance of a **Control Wizard**.

How to Manually Work with a Control (Generalized Procedure)

Step 1.   If the **Control Wizard** is enabled and you wish to work with a control manually, disable the wizard by selecting it.

Step 2.   Select the desired control from the **Control Toolbar**.

Step 3.   Draw the control onto the report.

Step 4.   Adjust control properties by entering **Edit Mode** (for controls that display captions), or adjust control formatting properties by selecting commands from the **Formatting** toolbar, or adjust control properties by using the **Property Sheet**.

Text Box Control

The **Text Box** control is used to display text. It can display a single line or multiple lines and is therefore a good candidate for displaying field values from a *Memo* field.

Text Boxes are generally used for two purposes on a report:

▪ As a bound control, they display field data in an underlying field from the report's record source.

▪ As a calculated control, they display the result of an expression. In this mode, the Control Source property (or the displayed text within the Text Box) must begin with an equals sign (=). General aspects of calculated controls are discussed in Chapter 7. Placement of calculated controls on reports is discussed on page 228.

When you add a Text Box to a report, it includes an attached label. This label may be removed from the **Text Box**, if desired, by selecting it separately from the Text Box and pressing the *Delete* key.

Important Text Box Control Properties

Property	Description
Control Source	Names the field if the control is bound, or contains an *expression* if the field is unbound. Expressions must always begin with an ***equals sign*** (=).
Running Sum	Controls whether a text box can store data across groups or across the entire report in order to produce running totals.
Format	Controls how the data are displayed in the text box. This property is useful for formatting numeric data.
Can Grow	Controls whether the Text Box can increase in size vertically in order to fully display its contents when the report is printed.
Can Shrink	Controls whether the Text Box can decrease in size vertically to best fit its contents when the report is printed.

When a Text Box is selected you can adjust many format properties by using controls on the **Formatting toolbar.**

Double-clicking on a Text Box control enters **Edit Mode**. In this mode you can enter, edit or delete the text displayed in the Text Box. Note that this action modifies the Text Box control's **Control Source** property.

Page Break Control

This control forces a page break where it is located on either a form or a report. There are properties of some of the form (and report) components such as the **Detail** area, that may also manage how a form or report appears on the printed page (for example, see the discussion of the **Keep Group Together** property, beginning on page 230). Nonetheless there may be times when you need to force an absolute page break and this control achieves that purpose. **Page Break** controls are unbound and contain very few properties. The **Page Break** control only affects the way a report behaves when printed, or when viewed in **Print Preview**.

How to Work with the Page Break Control

This procedure assumes that you have printed your report or have used **Print Preview** to identify where page breaks are required. You must be in **Report Design View** to use this control.

Step 1.   From the **Controls** group, select the **Page Break** control.

Step 2.   At the location on your report which requires a page break, place the **Page Break** control.

The **Page Break** control cannot be resized nor repositioned horizontally. It appears as a very short line to the extreme left margin of the form area. You may move the control vertically if desired.

The **Page Break** control has very few properties. *Top* specifies its vertical placement (relative to the top, left corner of the current form area). *Name* specifies a name for the control.

Subreport Control

The **Subreport Control** behaves identically like the **Subform Control**, the only difference being whether the control is placed on a form or a report. This control may be associated with the **Control Wizard** which makes management of the linking properties easier. Working with the control, in the context of a form, was discussed in detail beginning on page 110 so in this section we will discuss their use in the context of reports.

A central difference between the **Subform/Subreport control** is that its use is required when you wish to display related data on a form (modeling either a one-to-many or a many-to-many relationship). Reports don't necessarily have this requirement as grouping (discussed in Chapters 9, 10, and 13) manages the display of related data easily and without the need for a **Subreport**.

Subreports do make sense however if you are creating a report that pulls related data from several sources. For example, consider the following relational diagram:

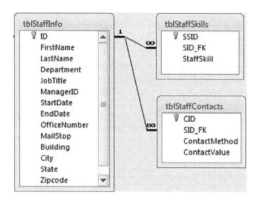

If you needed to create a report that, for each staff member, listed their skills as well as their contact information an approach using one or more **Subreport** controls would be preferred over an approach using grouping. This is because grouping makes sense in the context of a single one-to-many or many-to-many relationship but not multiple one-to-many or many-to-many relationships.

There would be two basic approaches to creating a report as described above:

- Create a simple grouped report that grouped *Staff Skills* by *staff ID*. Staff skills would be displayed in the **Detail** section, bracketed by a group **Header** and/or **Footer** based on *Staff ID*. You would place a **Subreport** based on the *Staff Contacts* table in one of two locations: The *ID* **Group Header** in order to print contact information *before* printing skills, or the *ID* **Group Footer** if you wish the contact information to be printed *after* skills. The **Subreport** should not be placed in the **Detail** section, otherwise staff contact information would print after every instance of staff skills.

- Create a simple report based on *Staff Information* and include two separate **Subreport Controls** - one bound to the *Staff Skills* table and the other one bound to *Staff Contacts*. The **Subreport** controls would be placed in the **Detail** section (there would be no group headers or footers that would apply in this situation) and the order of presentation of the grouped data would depend upon the physical location of the two **Subreport** controls.

The two approaches above would yield similar printed results. From a future maintenance perspective creating two separate **Subreports** yields more objects but potentially would be easier for a future developer to understand if the report required modification.

Certainly, when working with reports that require more than 2 sets of related joins, working with **Subreports** is a requirement. Grouping, as previously mentioned, works best with a single related thread between tables.

Chapter 13 | Grouped Reports and Calculated Controls

Overview of Grouped Reports

Reports are far more powerful than forms when it comes to displaying data in related groups. In a grouped report, you can set various grouping levels (up to 10). The report will automatically arrange or group related records using this scheme. The overall organization of a grouped report was first discussed on page 200.

For each group you create, a **Group Header** and **Group Footer** may be displayed. The header and footer sections are used to provide labels and formatting controls to assist in organizing the report. Most important, however, **Group Headers** and **Group Footers** are used to place *calculated controls* that summarize records contained within the group.

Points on Grouped Reports

- A report may be based on a single table and still contain groups. In an Employees table, you can group on fields within that table, such as by Department.

- When a report is based on two or more related tables, grouping usually is established to display records from the one side of the join as at least one of the groups. Related records from the table or tables on the many side of the join are displayed nested within the group.

- Regardless of the number of grouping levels, the lowest (or most nested) level is the report's Detail section. All other grouping levels headers and footers step symmetrically out from the Detail section.

- For any given grouping level, you can control the visibility of the Header and Footer, arrange sorting order, and specify how a group behaves at a page boundary.

- When using calculated controls to summarize grouped data, placement of the control on the report has important implications regarding function. The Detail section only "sees" one record at a time and is therefore not an appropriate location for a summary control. Each Group Header or Footer "sees" the entire set of records that will belong to that group. Finally, the Report Header and Footer "sees" the entire body of all records which will appear on the report.

- Page Headers and Footers only appear as a result of page boundaries. Conceptually, if you printed a report on a continuous sheet of paper, the controls in a Page Header and/or Page Footer section would each appear only once, at the top of the page for the **Page Header** and at the bottom of the printed report for the **Page Footer**. Page Headers and Footers are the only sections to interrupt Group Headers and Footers and the Detail section, and they only interrupt as a result of a page break.

Overview of Calculated Controls

You may recall from Chapter 7 that both forms and reports may contain calculated controls. These are generally text boxes (although a few other controls can be configured to be a calculated control) that are unbound and instead use an expression as its **Control Source** property. As with calculated controls on forms, these objects may refer to system information (such as today's date), built-in functions (like SUM or AVERAGE), values of other controls on the report, or domain aggregate functions.

As discussed in previous chapters, the central difference between forms and reports involves the latter's ability to contain groups with associated headers and/or footers. Placing a calculated control within the detail section, or a group header or footer will dictate the scope of the records that the calculated control will act upon. We will discuss grouping and then provide an example of the use of calculated controls in various report sections.

How Grouping Works

Understanding how grouping works is central to creating efficient and accurate reports (especially when working with calculated controls).

Single-Table Grouped Report

Consider the following recordset, derived from a single table, *StaffInfo*. For display purposes, the table has been sorted on the *Department* field.

Department	LastName	FirstName	JobTitle
Finance	Smith	Amanda	Director
Finance	Jones	Robert	Analyst II
Finance	Green	Tonya	Analyst II
Finance	McDonald	Michael	Analyst III
IT	DeLuca	Leon	Programmer
IT	Michaels	John	Programmer
IT	Palmer	Susan	Webmaster
IT	Kidwell	Michael	Director
IT	Jones	Jennifer	Support Tech
IT	Baseman	Tyrone	Support Tech
Management	Oltman	Greg	Director
Management	Regal	Cindy	Asst Director

If a grouped report were created based on this table, and a grouping level on *Department* were established, the report in **Print Preview** would appear similar to the following:

Department	LastName	FirstName	JobTitle
Staff by Department			
Finance			
	Green	Tonya	Analyst II
	Jones	Robert	Analyst II
	McDonald	Michael	Analyst III
	Smith	Amanda	Director
IT			
	Baseman	Tyrone	Support Tech
	DeLuca	Leon	Programmer
	Jones	Jennifer	Support Tech
	Kidwell	Michael	Director
	Michaels	John	Programmer
	Palmer	Susan	Webmaster
Management			
	Oltman	Greg	Director
	Ramsey	John	HR Manager

The report, viewed in **Report Design View** would appear similar to the following:

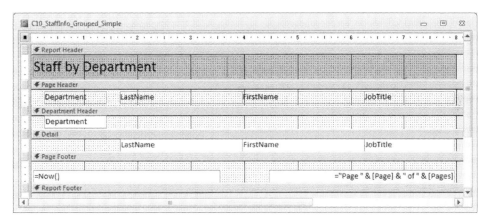

Considering just the **Department Header** and the **Detail** section of this grouped, one table report:

- For each Department, the report cycles through the employees within that department.

- For each employee within the current department, his or her record is processed in the report's Detail section.

- Thus the Detail section only "sees" one record at a time (the current employee record for the current department).

- The Department Header "sees" all the employee records for that department. Thus, if you needed to summarize data by department (for example, to produce a count of employees for each department), the calculated control would be located in either the Department Header, or if visible, the Department Footer section.

Multiple-Table Grouped Report

In the next example, a report is based on three tables, *tblStaffInfo*, *tblStaffandProjects*, and *tblProjects* (the middle, or *bridge* table) serves to relate the first and third tables together in a many-to-many relationship). The *many-to-many* join reflects the fact that each project may have zero to many staff assigned to it and each staff may, over time, be assigned to zero or more projects. The department information is obviously stored in the *tblStaffInfo* table and we need a single fact from the bridge table (*tblStaffandProjects*) - the budget information. In this database we assume that each staff are given individual budgets when tasked to a project, thus the budget for any staff member/project combination is located in the bridge table which basically stores the facts related to a staff-project assignment. Further, we'll assume that management is planning on an across-the-board adjustment of 110% of each project budget to account for increased costs so the report must also contain calculated controls to achieve this projection. An abbreviated view of the query that the Report Wizard would use to create this report would appear similar to the following.

LastName	Department	Budget	ProjectName
Smith	Finance	$10,000.00	VOIP migration
Smith	Finance	$95,000.00	Financial System Reengineering
Smith	Finance	$15,000.00	Six Sigma Implementation
Jones	Finance	$500.00	Server upgrade
Jones	Finance	$1,000.00	Financial System Reengineering
Jones	Finance	$2,500.00	Marketing Survey
Green	Finance	$500.00	Website upgrade
McDonald	Finance	$1,000.00	Financial System Reengineering
McDonald	Finance	$7,500.00	Cloud Storage Implementation
DeLuca	IT	$7,500.00	VOIP migration
DeLuca	IT	$7,500.00	Financial System Reengineering
Michaels	IT	$4,000.00	Website upgrade
Michaels	IT	$7,500.00	Six Sigma Implementation
Palmer	IT	$7,500.00	Server upgrade
Palmer	IT	$4,000.00	Website upgrade
Palmer	IT	$15,000.00	Cloud Storage Implementation

A summary report based on this query, and grouped first by *Project* and then by *Department* would appear similar to the following:

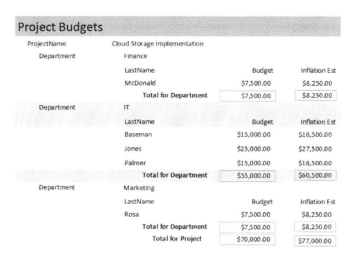

This report includes calculated controls to summarize *budget* costs and to calculate inflation adjustments for each department and for the project. There is a calculated control in the **Report Footer** to produce a grand total of all project budgets as well as to calculate a grand total for the inflation adjustments. The previous report would appear in **Report Design View** similar to the following:

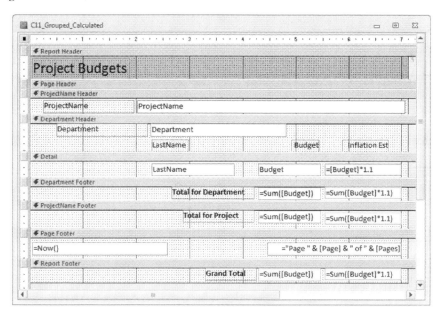

Considering the overall structure of this grouped, multiple-table report:

- For each Project, the report cycles first through each department associated with that project, and while processing a department, cycles through the staff from that department assigned to the current project. The facts about the staff-project assignment (including staff last name and their assigned budget for the project) constitute the **Detail** records, or the lowest level of detail in the report.

- At the level of the **Detail** section, the bound control *Budget* presents the amount budgeted to each staff for that particular project. A calculated control contains the expression *=[Budget] * 1.1* to calculate a 10% increase in the budgeted amount.

- At the level of the *Department* group, the group footer and header "see" all of the staff records, including their individual budgets, for the current department and the current project. A calculated control containing the expression *=SUM([Budget])* sums the total project budget for the current department and current project. Another calculated control contains the expression *=SUM([Budget] * 1.1)* to calculate the 10% budget increase for the current department and current project.

- Likewise, at the level of the *ProjectName* group, the group footer contains two controls, each containing the two expressions just discussed. At this level however, the calculated controls "see" all budget data across all departments for the current project, and thus provide total budget and total projected budget for the current project.

- The broadest view in the report is "seen" by the Report Header and Report Footer sections. Placing calculated controls in the Report Footer that contain the same two expressions discussed in the two previous paragraphs would yield grand totals for all project budgets and for all project budget projections of 10% above current budget amounts.

The following table outlines the expressions used by the controls in the various sections of the report illustrated on the previous pages. The topic of creating calculated controls and samples of expressions are presented starting on page 160. Remember that expressions are contained within a control's **Row Source** property.

Control/Placement	Expression
Display the amount each staff has been budgeted for the current project (Detail Section)	Budget (note that this isn't a calculated control, it is bound to a field named *Budget*.
Display a 10% projection of each staff's budget (Detail Section)	=[Budget] * 1.1
Tally the total project budget for each department for a given project (Department Footer)	=SUM([Budget])
Project the total project budget for each department for a given project (Department footer)	=SUM([Budget] * 1.1)
Total the budget for each project (ProjectName Footer)	=SUM([Budget])
Project each project total budget by 10% (ProjectName Footer)	=SUM([Budget] * 1.1)
Display a grand total of all project budgets across all departments (Report Footer)	=SUM([Budget])
Take the grand total of all project budgets and project by 10% (Report Footer)	=SUM([Budget] * 1.1)

Creating a Grouped Report

The task of using a **Report Wizard** to create a grouped report was discussed on page 185. The discussion in this section focuses on creating a grouped report working directly in **Report Design View**. Note that you would use these methods to modify a grouped report created using a **Report Wizard**.

When creating a grouped report on a single table, you simply indicate that the table will serve as the report's record source. For multiple-table reports, you must first create a query to gather the desired fields from the target tables. The report then uses the query as its record source.

How to Create a Grouped Report Using Report Design View

This is a generalized procedure for manually creating a grouped report.

Step 1.   If you wish to create a report based on two or more tables, first create a query that gathers the desired fields from the target tables. Save your query design.

Step 2.   From the **Create** tab, in the **Reports** group, choose **Report Design**. The report will open in **Report Design View**.

Step 3.   Open the **Property Sheet** for the report and attach a table or query to the report's **Record Source** property. This will bind the report to data.

Step 4.   To establish groups, use the **Group, Sort, and Total** control. This facility will also control **Group Header** and **Footer** visibility. The **Group, Sort, and Total** control is discussed in the next section.

Step 5.   Use the **Field List** to drag bound controls onto the report. Placement of the controls within various sections is important for the report to work properly. In general, ensure that the fields are placed within the appropriate **Group Header** if the field describes something about the group, or in the report's **Detail** section if the field contains the lowest level (non-repeating) values from the table or query.

Step 6.   If calculated controls are desired, place them in the appropriate **Group Header** or **Footer**, **Detail** section, or **Report Header** or **Footer**, depending upon the type of summary you desire. Placement of calculated controls is discussed on page 228.

Step 7.   Adjust any other formatting attributes of the report and its controls, as desired.

Step 8.   View your report in **Print Preview** and verify that it is grouping data correctly, and in the case of calculated controls, that they are performing as expected. Return to **Report Design View** if needed and make any corrections or adjustments.

Step 9.   Save the design of your report.

Group, Sort, and Total

The **Group, Sort, and Total** window manages all aspects of the grouping levels in a report. You use this window to manually establish each group, and for each group the window is used to control **Header** and **Footer** visibility, sorting order, and how a group behaves at a page break. This control is also helpful for managing grouping when working with a grouped report created by the Report Wizard. Unlike other windows in **Design View**, this window is fixed at the bottom of the **Report Design View** window. It may be opened or closed but not relocated.

How to Use the Group, Sort, and Total Control

The report should be open in **Report Design View**. Although this window is available in **Report Layout View**, you cannot see the various headers and footers required to accurately place various bound and unbound controls.

Step 1.   From the **Report Design Tools** tab, in the **Grouping & Totals** toolbar, select **Group & Sort**. The window will appear at the bottom of the **Report Design View** similar to the following:

Step 2.   If desired, choose **More >** to display the full set of group, sort, and total options. Use the following table as a guide.

Option	Description
Group on	Lists the field to group on. The sorting and **By entire value** options will change depending upon the data type of the grouping field.
With A on Top	Sort options include alphabetical (A-Z) or reverse (Z-A). Text fields only.
From smallest to largest	Numeric sort options - either smallest to largest or reverse order.
From oldest to newest	Date/Time sort options - either oldest to newest or newest to oldest.
By entire value	Sets what constitutes a group. For text use the entire field value or the first *n* characters. For numbers, group by entire value or in sets of 5's, 10's, etc. For date/time you can group by the entire value, or cluster dates within years, months, days, etc.
With no totals	Determines whether any calculated controls will be placed on the report. You specify the field to total, the function to be applied (Sum, Average, etc) and the location of the totals control.
With title *value*	Sets the contents of a label control which will appear in the current group header.
With a header section	Controls **Group Header** visibility.
Without a footer section	Controls **Group Footer** visibility.
Do not keep group together on one page	Sets how grouped data behave at a page break. You can elect to keep all data within a group on a single page (if possible), or to print the group header and the first detail record prior to a page break. The default is to not attempt to keep grouped data on the same page.

Step 3.   To add an additional group, select **Add a group**, then adjust the group properties using the previous table as a guide.

Step 4.   If desired, arrange the grouping order by using the **Move Up** or **Move Down** controls - located at the far right top of the **Group, Sort, and Total** control. As you move a group's location within the control the corresponding group header and footer sections will change position on the report.

Step 5.   If desired, add a field to sort on by choosing **Add a sort**. This affects the sorting of records in the **Detail** section of the report.

As an example, the report created beginning on page 226 would display a **Group, Sort & Total** window similar to the following:

How to Add or Remove a Group Header or Footer

The **Group, Sort & Total** window is used to add or remove a group header or footer. If not visible, show the **Group, Sort & Total** window by selecting it from the **Grouping & Totals** group on the **Design** tab.

Step 1.   Click on the desired **Group On**, then choose **More >**.

Step 2.   Toggle the desired **With/Without a Header** or **With/Without a Footer** control.

 Warning: If controls are present in a **Header** or **Footer**, removing that section will remove the controls as well.

 The **Group, Sort & Total** window does not control **Page** or **Report Headers** and/or **Footers** (except if you add a Grand Total control then a **Report Footer** is created). To control visibility of **Page** or **Report** headers or footers, right-click on an existing **Header** or **Footer** title bar, or on the **Detail** title bar and choose the appropriate action from the shortcut menu.

How to Control Sort Order

The **Group, Sort & Total** window is used to establish up to 4 sort orders at the level of the **Detail** section. To control sorting within a group refer to the previous procedure.

Step 1.   If not visible, open the **Group, Sort & Total** window.

Step 2.   Select the **Add a sort** control.

Step 3.   Select the field to sort on from the list of fields bound to the report, then choose a sort order.

Step 4.   Repeat Steps 2 and 3 to add additional sort orders.

 When defining multiple sorts, adjust the order of sorted fields by using the **Move Up** or **Move Down** controls - located to the extreme right of the currently-selected sort bar.

 If you sort on a field that is also a group level, any sorting order applied to the group control overrides sorting defined specifically for the field. Sorting makes most sense when applied to fields contained within the **Detail** section of the report.

Chapter 14 | Special Report Topics

We consider two specialty report types in this chapter: unbound reports and mailing label reports. The former are generally used to augment other reports while the latter support generation of mailing labels for bulk mail operations.

Unbound Reports

An unbound report by itself cannot display any data since, by definition, its **Record Source** property is blank. There are two general reasons you may want to work with an unbound report:

- To serve as a cover or an appendix to a bound report. In this context you would add one or more text boxes or labels to contain the desired content.

- To act as a container for subreports which *are* bound to data. By embedding one or more **Subreport** controls on an unbound report, their data would be displayed when the unbound report is printed or previewed. The content of each **Subreport** control would fully print and would appear in the same physical order as the placement of the **Subreport** controls on the unbound report. This behavior is in contrast to the way that a bound, grouped report would behave.

How to Create an Unbound Report

Creation of this type of report is always manual. There is no wizard for unbound reports.

Step 1.　　From the **Reports** group on the **Create** tab, choose **Blank Report**. An unbound report will appear in **Report Layout View**. By default the report will contain a **Page Header** and **Page Footer**, as well as the mandatory **Detail** section.

Step 2.　　If you require a **Report Header** and/or **Report Footer**, switch to **Report Design View** and follow the procedure beginning on page 203.

Step 3.　　Add any desired controls. Recall that the only bound control type supported would be a **Subreport** control. You may place calculated controls on an unbound report, although they may only refer to system functions or domain aggregate functions. For example, to display the system date and time.

If you need to add text to an unbound report, you have two options: the **Text Box** or the **Label** control. In the former, you add text by enclosing it in double quotes and beginning with an *equals sign* (=). In the latter case you simply type the desired text within the label.

Mailing Label Reports

You can create labels formatted for a wide variety of label types using the **Label Wizard**. Alternatively, you can create custom label reports. Generally mailing labels are created using the **Wizard** as Microsoft Access ships with an extensive library of commercial mailing label types (40 vendors and hundreds of label products are represented).

How to Create a Label Report using the Label Wizard

This procedure focuses on using the **Label Wizard** and commercially-available labels. The following section discusses the creation of a custom size label.

Step 1.   From the **Reports** group on the **Create** tab, choose **Labels**. The first dialog box of the **Label Wizard** will appear similar to the following:

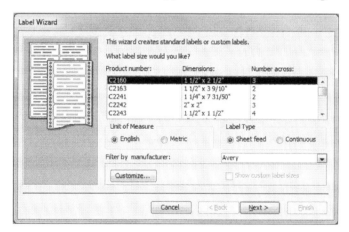

Step 2.   Use the **Filter by manufacturer** drop down box to choose the desired vendor.

Step 3.   If working with a continuous feed printer, select **Continuous** from the **Label Type** area.

Step 4.   Adjust the **Unit of Measure** if required.

Step 5.   Select the desired label product from the list in the **What label size would you like?** list box. Choose **Next** when ready. The second dialog box of the **Label Wizard** will appear similar to the following:

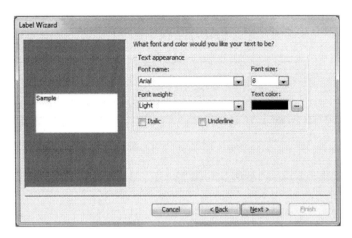

Step 6.   Adjust any font attributes, as desired. Choose **Next** when done. The next dialog box will appear as:

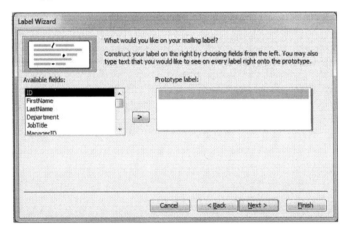

Step 7.   Use the **Available Fields** list to place the desired fields onto the **Prototype Label**. When required you must manually enter a *Space* between data fields (for example, between *FirstName* and *LastName* fields). Use the *Return* key to create a new line on the prototype. An example of a completed mailing label would appear similar to the following:

 The amount of space available on your label (both in terms of width and the number of lines of text) is a direct function of the label size you selected in Step 5 and any font options you choose in Step 6. If the prototype label is too small, use the **Back** button and adjust font attributes or choose another label size.

Step 8.   Once your **Prototype Label** has been created, choose **Next**. In the next dialog box, select one or more fields to sort your labels by. For example, in the United States, bulk mailing discounts require that mail be sorted by zip code. Choose **Next** when ready.

Step 9.   In the last dialog box of the **Label Wizard**, provide a name for your label report and choose whether to open the report in **Report View** or **Report Design View**. Select **Finish** to end the process.

A completed mailing label report would appear similar to the following when viewed in **Print Preview** (when viewing a multi-column report in **Report View** you do not see multiple columns):

The label report, when viewed in **Report Design View** would appear as:

From the previous illustration you can see how the **Label Wizard** inserts blank spaces, commas, and new lines. Anything typed by you is converted into a *literal expression* while using the ***Enter*** key results in the creation of a new text box, stacked below existing text boxes.

Important Label Report Properties (Page Setup Tab)

Property	Description
Margins (Page Setup)	Sets the page margins for the label report. For many label styles, these values will be significantly smaller than for standard reports.
Number of Columns (Page Setup)	Specifies the number of columns in the label report.
Row Spacing (Page Setup)	Sets the amount of blank space between rows.
Column Spacing (Page Setup)	Specifies the amount of space between columns. This setting is analogous to *gutters* in desktop publishing applications.
Column Size (Page Setup)	Sets the **Height** and **Width** of each column. The **Height** property is the same as the **Height** property of the **Detail** section, while the **Width** property is the same as the report's **Width** property.

When working with multicolumn label reports, think of the report in **Report Design View** as being a template that is applied to the printed page via the column settings as specified in the **Page Setup** dialog box. You can see this difference by toggling between **Report** and **Print Preview** views.

How to Create a Custom Label Report

A mailing label report can be a complex object as multicolumn reports require careful adjustment of right, left, and internal margins in order to synchronize printout with your label stock. Nonetheless, there may be cases where you need to manually create a label report rather than utilize the **Label Report Wizard**.

When you create a custom label Access prompts you for a name for the label. Once created your custom label is available to all databases managed on the computer used to establish the custom label.

Step 1.   From the **Reports** group on the **Create** tab, choose **Labels**.

Step 2.   On the first dialog box, select **Customize...** The New Label Size dialog box will appear as follows:

Step 3.   Choose **New** to create a new label. The **New Label** dialog box will appear similar to the following:

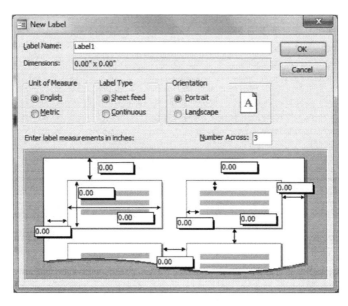

Step 4.　Enter a name for your custom label, select the **Unit of Measure**, **Label Type**, and print **Orientation**. Note that the **Dimensions** text area will display data as you complete the next step.

Step 5.　Move to the **Enter label measurements** area and use the following table to complete your custom label measurements.

Position within preview window	Measurement
Upper left	These four measurements include top (and although not illustrated, bottom) and left margin and label height and width. The margins are the distance from the physical edge of the page to the beginning of the label area. The label height and width are the physical extents of the label printed area.
Upper right	Two of the four measurements in this area are the internal margins for your label. If you wish to be able to fully utilize the area specified as label height and width, leave these values at zero, otherwise use these controls to specify an internal margin or gutter for your label. The right-most measure is the right margin for the printed page. The last measure within this group is the blank spacing (if any) between labels within the column of labels.
Lower center	If working with a multicolumn label report, this last measure is the horizontal spacing between columns. Leave at zero for single-column reports.

Step 6.　When your new label name and dimensions have been specified, select **OK**. If there are errors in your specifications (such as total horizontal dimensions not adding up), Access will inform you of the error and place the focus in one of

the dimension boxes that must be addressed. Continue correcting errors as necessary until Access closes the **New Label** dialog box.

Step 7.   Close the **New Label Size** dialog box by selecting **Close**.

Step 8.   Once you have returned to the first dialog box of the **Label Wizard**, continue with Step 6 from the previous procedure.

Working with Custom Labels

Once you have created a custom label, you can select it for printing, make changes to the specifications, or copy it to use as the basis for a new label definition.

Step 1.   From the **Reports** group on the **Create** tab, choose **Labels**.

Step 2.   On the first dialog box, select **Customize...** Use the following table to determine the next action.

Option	Procedure
Print a custom label	Select the custom label from the list in the **Label name** area, then choose **Close**. Proceed as if working with a commercially-available label.
Delete a custom label	Select the label from the list in the **Label name** area, then choose **Delete**.
Modify a custom label	Select the label and then choose **Edit**. Proceed with Step 4 from the previous procedure.
Copy a custom label	Select the label and then choose **Duplicate**. Proceed with Step 4 from the previous procedure.

Appendix A | Staff and Projects Database

The samples in this manual illustrate a simple staff and projects database – a design that might commonly be used in an organization that tracks information about staff (contact methods and skills) as well as information about projects (here the main interest is in the staffing of projects as well as the budget for a project). A copy of this database may be downloaded from www.sycamoretechnicalpress.com

The basic relationships between the tables used in the sample database appear in the following illustration.

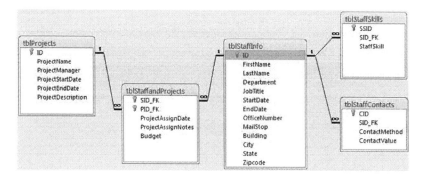

The structure of the 5 tables, and if applicable, the indices used to maintain uniqueness among rows, are presented below.

tblStaffInfo

This table, along with tblProjects, can be considered the two main tables in the staff and projects database. A primary key affords an easy way to relate a staff record to other tables and an index based on staff first and last name as well as department enforce uniqueness for each row.

Field Name	Data Type	Description
ID	AutoNumber	Primary Key
FirstName	Text	
LastName	Text	
Department	Text	
JobTitle	Text	
StartDate	Date/Time	
EndDate	Date/Time	
OfficeNumber	Text	
MailStop	Text	
Building	Text	
City	Text	

There are two indices for tblStaffInfo. The primary key is automatically created by Access. The index **Staff** asserts that no two records may contain the same staff first and last name and department.

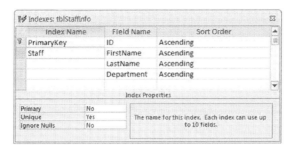

tblProjects

Along with tblStaffInfo this table constitutes the other major table in the Staff and Projects database. Both tables store information about the two realms the database focuses on. Like the tblStaffInfo table, a second index **Project** enforces uniqueness by assuming the combination of project name, project manager, and start date will not be repeated.

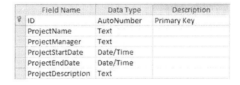

The indexes for tblProjects appears as:

tblStaffContact

This table relates the one-to-many ways you can contact each staff member. An index based on the foreign key for the staff ID, the contact method, and the contact value, ensure that no two rows are duplicated.

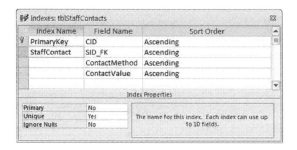

The index appears as follows:

tblStaffSkills

Similar to tblStaffContacts, this table stores any skills associated with each staff member.

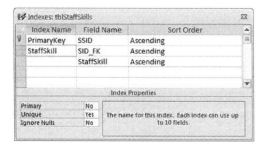

The index, based on the staff foreign key and staff skill, ensures uniqueness for each row:

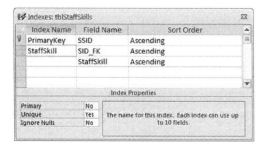

tblStaffandProjects

The final table is the only bridge table in this design. Its purpose is to manage the information that relates to project staffing. Each project may have one or more staff assigned to it, and ultimately, each staff member may be assigned to zero or more projects. It is also the only table in the database design to utilize two fields which together make up the table's primary key: the foreign key to the tblStaffInfo primary key and the foreign key to the tblProjects primary key. Using these two fields together ensures uniqueness among the rows and enforces the logical requirement that no staff can be assigned to a project more than once. This simple design removes any requirement for an additional index to enforce uniqueness among the records.

Further, in this design the budget field implies that each staff member is given an individual budget for their part in a project. Recall from the discussion on banded reports that even given this configuration, with a project staffed by several members from the same department, one can easily generate a report that groups project staffing information by department, with the purpose of providing totals of the budget amount both by staff, by department, and by project.

Field Name	Data Type	Description
SID_FK	Number	Foreign key to tblStaffInfo primary key
PID_FK	Number	Foreign key to tblProjects primary key
ProjectAssignDate	Date/Time	
ProjectAssignNotes	Memo	
Budget	Currency	

Appendix B | Macros

Macros are a form of automation used by Microsoft Access in several ways. When you create a **Command Button** using the **Command Button Wizard** (discussed on page 117), the wizard implements the automation action as a macro. You may also create macros separately (they are a category of objects within a Microsoft Access database) and run them as independent automation objects or, like the **Command Button Wizard**, bind the macro to a specific event associated with a form, report, or their contained controls.

A full description of macros is beyond the scope of this book, and a discussion of the events which are associated with Forms, Reports, and their controls is detailed in the book in this series, *Building VBA Applications using Microsoft Access 2010*. In this Appendix we will conduct an overview tour of macros and the editor used to create or edit them.

This Appendix does not discuss **Data Macros**, which are macros coupled to specific events associated with data entry, editing, or deletion in a table. **Data Macros** are created and managed using the **Table** tab when a table is open in **Table Datasheet View**.

Points on Macros

- You can create a macro using the **Macro Builder** and run it as an object from the **Navigation Pane**, or attach it to an event on a form or report (or any of their contained controls).

- If you use the **Command Button Wizard** to elicit some action, a macro is created but it remains embedded within the control. It will not appear in the list of macros on the **Navigation Pane**, but if you select the *Click* event on the **Events** tab of the **Property Sheet** for the **Command Button**, the macro code will appear in the **Macro Editor**.

- A macro that elicits a common action in your database is best managed by creating it as a single macro object and attaching it to the forms or reports, or their contained controls, as needed.

- Microsoft Access 2010 contains more macro actions than previous versions, in part to assist users in creating useful automation without having to learn VBA (Visual Basic for Applications) code. Many of these macros conduct what Microsoft refers to as *dangerous* actions, such as deleting objects from your database. The **Macro Editor** can distinguish between the "safe" and "dangerous" actions and you can modify the editor to view or hide the dangerous macro actions.

- Unless you specifically grant permission to run macros, Access will fail to execute macros you create. To enable macros in your database, from the **File** menu, choose **Options**, and then

Trust Center. Select **Trust Center Settings…**, choose **Macro Settings**, and enable macros by choosing **Enable All Macros**, or **Disable all macros except digitally signed macros** (the latter assumes you have access to the self certification creator).

 SelfCert.exe allows you to create a digital security certificate that will permit you to run all macros in all members of the Microsoft Office suite, but only on your computer. Other users who share your applications will still be challenged to permit or deny executable macros and/or code. To create a self certificate, from the **Start** menu, follow this path: All Programs> Microsoft Office> Microsoft Office *<version>* Tools> Digital Certificate for VBA Projects

An Introduction to the Macro Editor

This editing facility appears when you select **Macro** from the **Create** tab, or when you choose the **Macro Builder** from any event on the **Event** tab of the **Property Sheet** for the currently-selected object. In these procedures we will assume that a macro is being created from the **Create** tab.

The editor presents all of the macro actions and *program flow* elements you'll need to create a useful macro. The **Macro Editor** and the **Action Catalog** appear similar to the following:

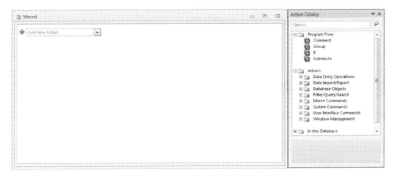

Macro Design Tools Tab

Group	Description
Tools	Commands to run the current macro, either uninterrupted or a step at a time, or to convert the current macro to VBA code.
Collapse/Expand	Expand or collapse only the actions in the current macro or expand or collapse all macro elements.
Show/Hide	Toggle the display of the **Action Catalog** and/or display or hide the macros deemed not safe to run in an untrusted database.

Macro Editor Components

Window/Component	Description
Editor / Add New Action	Lists all possible actions from the Action Catalog. As you select a specific command, additional arguments may appear. For macros that contain two or more actions, program flow elements, or comments, these appear vertically arranged indicating the order of execution when the macro is run.
Action Catalog	Organizes and displays all macro elements, grouped into **Program Flow**, **Actions**, and other macros in the current database.

Program Flow in a Macro

Macros run in one of two modes. In the simplest case the macro executes one or more actions sequentially. For macros that contain two or more actions, the order of processing is from the topmost action downward (as they appear listed in the **Macro Editor**).

A slightly more complex version involves one or more **IF..THEN..END IF** logic blocks. There are several variations on this type of program flow but the key to understanding them is to note that program flow will either enter or bypass an **IF..THEN..END IF** block depending upon whether the initial *conditional statement* associated with the **IF** statement resolves to *True*. If the conditional statement resolves to true then any macro code between the **IF** and the ending **END IF** block is executed (although you may nest **IF..END IF** blocks within one another). The variations on an **IF..ENDIF** block are explained in the following table.

Logic Block	Description

IF *conditional statement* THEN
  ActionStatement
END IF
	The simplest of the logic blocks. If the conditional statement resolves to *True* then ActionStatement (or statements) is/are run, otherwise program flow bypasses the action statement and continues with any macro statements below the END IF block terminator.

IF *conditional statement* THEN
  ActionStatement1
ELSE
  ActionStatement2
END IF
	As above except that if the conditional statement isn't true, ActionStatement2 is run. In this example either ActionStatement1 or ActionStatement2 runs.

IF *conditional statement* THEN
  ActionStatement1
ELSEIF *conditional statment2 THEN*
  ActionStatement2
END IF
	If the initial conditional statement is true, ActionStatement1 runs. Otherwise, if the conditional statement 2 is true, ActionStatement2 runs. If neither conditional statements resolve to true then no action statements run.

IF *conditional statement* THEN
  ActionStatement1
ELSEIF *conditional statment2 THEN*
  ActionStatement2
ELSE
  ActionStatment3
END IF
	As above, except the **ELSE** statement guarantees that ActionStatement3 will run if neither of the previous conditional statements resolve to true.

Action Statements

An action statement elicits some action from a macro. Action statements appear in two locations in the **Macro Editor**. You may choose an action statement by name from any drop down box with the *Add new action* prompt. Alternatively, use the **Action Catalog** to locate the desired action statement. The **Action Catalog** organizes action statements within functional categories.

Many action statements are associated with one or more *arguments*. Arguments help tailor the action statement so it works on a specific object. Other action statements, such as **Beep**, lack any arguments.

How to Create a Simple Macro

We will assume that one important function in your database is a routine export of table data into HTML format.

Step 1.   From the **Create** tab, in the **Macros & Code** group, choose **Macro**.

Step 2.   If the **Action Catalog** isn't visible, enable it by choosing **Action Catalog** from the **Design** tab.

Step 3.   Either use the **Add new action** drop down box, or navigate to the **Data Import/Export** folder on the **Action Catalog** and double click (or click and drag) the item **Export with Formatting**. Once the action has been added to the macro editor, it will appear as follows:

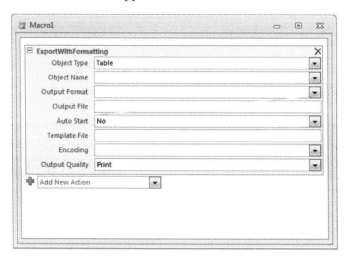

Step 4.   Complete the arguments (not all are required) to conduct the desired operation. In this case we will export a **Table** of the name **tblHRData**. The **Output Format** is **HTML** and the **Output File** is D:\Data\Backups\HRDataBackup.HTML. To open a browser once the export has been conducted you would select *Yes* for the **Auto Start** property.

Step 5.   Save your macro using the **Save** button on the **Quick Start** toolbar.

How to Create a Macro with a IF..END Block

We will expand on the previous macro example and make it conditional. The macro will only conduct the backup operation if the current day is Friday.

Step 1.   Create a macro using the previous example as a guide. Remain in the **Macro Editor**.

Step 2.   On the **Action Catalog**, open the **Program Flow** folder and either double click or drag an **IF** item to the editor. The **IF** and **END IF** blocks will appear *below* the **ExportWithFormatting** block. To insert this block *within* the **IF..END IF** block, select the **ExportWithFormatting** action statement and either drag it to just below the **IF** statement or use the **Move Down** arrow to place it between the **IF** and **END IF** statements.

Step 3. Select the **IF** statement and move to the **Conditional Expression** text area. Either use the **Expression Builder (...)** (discussed beginning on page 161) or manually enter the following expression:

Weekday(date()) =6

Step 4. Save your macro.

 The **Weekday()** function takes a required argument which must be a date and returns a number that indicates the day of the week for that date. Here, rather than pass a literal date we instead pass the **Date()** function which returns the current date. If the current day is a Friday the function will return **6**. If 6=6 (which is true!) the action statement between the **IF** and **END IF** block will run.

Running Macros

There are three ways to run a macro: From the **Navigation Pane**, from within the **Macro Editor**, or attached to an event associated with a form, report, or one of their embedded controls.

How to Run a Macro from the Navigation Pane

Step 1. Select the desired macro from the **Macro** area of the **Navigation Pane**.

Step 2. Either double-click on the macro, or right click and choose **Run** from the shortcut menu.

How to Run a Macro from the Macro Editor

Step 1. From the **Tools** group on the **Design** tab, select **Run**, or, to step through the macro, enable **Single Step** and then select **Run**.

How to Run a Macro Attached to an Event

In this example, we'll attach a macro named *macBackupHRData* to the **Close** event of a form that serves as a database's main menu. The intent is that this macro will run whenever the main menu form is closed.

Step 1. Open the desired form in **Form Design View**.

Step 2 Double-click on the **Form Selector** to open the **Property Sheet**, or alternatively, open the **Property Sheet** and if necessary, choose **Form** from the object list.

Step 3.   Select the **Events** tab, then click in the text area for the **On Close** event.

Step 4.   From the drop down box, select the desired macro.

Step 5.   Save the form design.

 Forms, reports, and their controls are rich with *events* such as **On Close**. Events are discussed in detail in the book *Building VBA Applications using Microsoft Access 2010*, which is part of this series.

Index

About the Author

F. Mark Schiavone was originally trained as a research scientist, and in that capacity he began constructing database applications and analyzing complex data sets over 30 years ago. His database skills include Microsoft Access, Microsoft SQL Server and MySQL and he has constructed applications using those platforms for clients in large to mid-size organizations, including the US Department of Education, the National Weather Service, and the International Monetary Fund. He has authored over 30 training titles in topics such as Microsoft Access, Microsoft Word, Microsoft Excel, and in the VBA programming language. He also has 8 years experience in public finance, capital project planning, and local government budgeting and has constructed numerous database applications to support those endeavors.

He has restored three stone houses (two of which were 18th century while the most recent house dates from 1835), reroofed a loafing barn, disassembled and reassembled a corn crib, and built several frame houses, additions or outbuildings. He has designed every new structure built on his property. He is a passionate all weather, high mileage motorcyclist and is usually the only motorcyclist on the local roads when the temperature is below 25° F.

87909310R00152

Made in the USA
Lexington, KY
03 May 2018